I0483108

What Mark Twain Learned Me 'bout Public Speakin'

Conor Cunneen

with help, inspiration and instruction from

Mark Twain

MMXIV

Suas Cork Books

DEDICATION and THANKS

This book is dedicated to everyone who enjoys the wit, humor, passion, pathos and storytelling of Mark Twain and is interested in some good ol' learnin'!

On reviewing my notes and ramblings while compiling this labor of love, (Twain is an easy man to love, especially from a distance) I eventually saw the light and said "Why rewrite the words of a genius? Let him speak for himself."

Twain wrote: *That is what a teaspoonful of brains will do for a man—and admirers had often told me I had nearly a basketful—though they were rather reserved as to the size of the basket.*

My basket is just about large enough to realize that I should let the man who was born Sam Clemens do the talking together with some contemporaries.

While better people than me have written magnificent analytic tomes on the famed humorist, my contribution is to provide an interpretation of what communicators can learn from Mark Twain and illustrate how I, as a professional speaker, attempt to implement all that learnin'!

Internal images are from the wonderful Mark Anderson unless otherwise stated. Thanks also to Dave Thomson for the cover image by Joseph Keppler from *PUCK*, Dec. 23, 1885. There is more material published on Mark Twain than any sane person could read, but I have to tip my hat in particular to Twainquotes.com which is quite simply a wonderful monument to the works and memory of a great man. I admit I checked it more than once.

Enjoy the learnin'!

Conor Cunneen

+++++++++

"LEARNING THE RIVER."

"When I say I'll learn ['Teach' is not in the river vocabulary] a man the river, I mean it. And you can depend on it, I'll learn him or kill him.'

Life on the Mississippi – Mark Twain
(Image: Life on the Mississippi, 1883)

What Mark Twain Learned Me 'bout Public Speakin'

Conor Cunneen

with help, inspiration and instruction from

Mark Twain

Cataloging-in-Publication Data

Cunneen, Conor

What Mark Twain Learned Me 'bout Public Speakin'/ Conor Cunneen

2014917286

Copyright © MMXIV

Suas Cork Books

www.IrishmanSpeaks.com

Mark Twain World Speaking Tour
1895 - 1896

JULY 1895

United States: Cleveland, Ohio * Sault Ste. Marie, Michigan * Mackinac, Michigan * Petoskey, Michigan * Duluth, Minnesota * Minneapolis, Minnesota * St. Paul, Minnesota * Winnipeg, Canada * Crookston, Minnesota * Great Falls, Montana

AUGUST

Butte, Montana * Anaconda, Montana * Helena, Montana * Missoula, Montana * Spokane, Washington * Portland, Oregon * Olympia, Washington * Tacoma, Washington * Seattle, Washington * New Whatcom, Washington * Vancouver, Canada * Victoria, Canada

SEPTEMBER

Fiji Islands: *"It is a fine race, the Fijians, with brains in their heads, and an inquiring turn of mind."*
Australia: *"You Australians seem to deserve the title of "the cordial nation."*
Sydney * Melbourne

OCTOBER

Adelaide * Horsham* Stawell * Ballarat * Bendigo * Maryborough* Melbourne * Geelong * Prahran

NOVEMBER

New Zealand: *"All people think that New Zealand is close to Australia or Asia, or somewhere, and that you cross to it on a bridge. But that is not so. It is not close to anything!"*

Invercargill * Dunedin * Timaru * Damaru * Christchurch * Auckland * Napier

DECEMBER

Palmerston North * Wanganui * Hawara * New Plymouth* Wellington *

Australia: Scone * Sydney * Melbourne * Adelaide * Glenelg

1896

JANUARY

India: *"India! The land of dreams and romance, of fabulous wealth and fabulous poverty, of splendor and rags, of palaces and hovels."*

Bombay * Poona * Baroda

FEBRUARY

Allahabad * Benares * Calcutta * Darjeeling * Muzaf-
farpur * Uttar Pradesh * Lucknow * Kanpur * Agra

MARCH

Jaipur * Delhi * Lahore * Rawalpindi *

CEYLON: *"What a dream it was of tropical splendors
of bloom and blossom, and Oriental conflagrations of
costume!"*
Colombo

APRIL

MAURITIUS: *"Apparently, there has been only one
prominent event in the history of Mauritius, and that
one didn't happen."*

MAY

SOUTH AFRICA: *"The splendid black satin skin of
the South African Zulus of Durban seemed to me to
come very close to perfection."*
Durban * Pietermaritzburg * Johannesburg * Pretoria
* Johannesburg

JUNE

Bloemfontein * Queenstown * Williams Town * East London * Port Elizabeth, * Grahamstown

JULY

Kimberly * Cape Town * Claremont

Twain departed Cape Town, July 15 arriving in Southampton England, July 31. The World Tour was over.

Mark Twain D.Litt, Oxford 1907

"A great ovation was reserved for Mark Twain, who was the lion of the occasion. Everyone rose when he was escorted up the aisle and he was applauded for a quarter of an hour. When Dr. Ingram Bywater, Regius Professor of Greek, presented the American humorist to the convocation, the students started a fire of chaff about his books and their heroes, mixed with frequent questions, such as "Where is your white suit?" Mark Twain said afterward that he wanted to reply, but was determined to observe the etiquette, which demands that recipients of degrees be silent."

The New York Times, June 27, 1907

Table of Contents

CHAPTER I

M - Message and Speech Preparation

Mark Twain studied every word and syllable, and memorized them by a system of mnemonics peculiar to himself.

William Dean Howells

1

I

What Mark Twain Learned me 'bout **Message and Speech Preparation**

- ◆ There is no substitute for preparation, rehearsal and practice
- ◆ To get an audience to "believe it is an impromptu speech—that is an art."
- ◆ Practice your material in front of smaller audiences

++++++++++ ++++++++++ ++++++++++

Mark Twain Speeches - Introduction by William D. Howells

I never heard Clemens speak when I thought he quite failed; some burst or spurt redeemed him when he seemed flagging short of the goal, and, whoever else was in the running, he came in ahead.

His near-failures were the error of a rare trust to the spontaneity in which other speakers confide, or are believed to confide, when they are on their feet. He knew that from the beginning of oratory the orator's spontaneity was for the silence and solitude of the closet where he mused his words to an imagined audience; that this was the use of orators from Demosthenes and Cicero up and down.

He studied every word and syllable, and memorized them by a system of mnemonics peculiar to himself, consisting of an arbitrary arrangement of things on a table—knives, forks, salt-cellars; inkstands, pens, boxes, or whatever was at hand—which stood for points and clauses and climaxes, and were at once

3

indelible diction and constant suggestion. He studied every tone and every gesture, and he forecast the result with the real audience from its result with that imagined audience. Therefore, it was beautiful to see him and to hear him; he rejoiced in the pleasure he gave and the blows of surprise which he dealt; and because he had his end in mind, he knew when to stop.

++++++++++

Mark Twain - A Biography: Albert Bigelow Paine

Early in the evenings, we (Twain and fellow speakers) scattered out among the towns and made them indicate the good and poor things in the new lectures........ And so, when we finally stepped on to the great stage at the Music Hall we already had the verdict in our pocket.

++++++++++

Mark Twain - A Biography: Albert Bigelow Paine

In the neighborhood of Boston there were other compensations. He could spend a good part of his days at the Lyceum headquarters, in School Street, where there was always congenial fellowship—Nasby, Josh Billings, and the rest of the peripatetic group that about the end of the year collected there. Their lectures were never tried immediately in Boston, but in the outlying towns; tried and perfected—or discarded. When the provincial audiences were finally satisfied, then the final test in the Boston Music Hall was made, and if this proved successful the rest of the season was safe.

++++++++++

Autobiography of Mark Twain

The performance began at a quarter past two, and I, number three in a list of ten (if we include the introducer), was not called to the bat until a quarter after three. My reading was ten minutes long. When I had selected it originally, it was twelve minutes long, and it had taken me a good hour to find ways of reducing it by two minutes without damaging it. I was through in ten minutes. Then I retired to my seat to enjoy the agonies of the audience. I did enjoy them for an hour or two; then all the cruelty in my nature was exhausted and my native humanity came to the front again. By half past five a third of the house was asleep; another third were dying; and the rest were dead. I got out the back way and went home.

++++++++++

Mark Twain Speeches: To the Whitefriars

But impromptu speaking—that is what I was trying to learn. That is a difficult thing. I used to do it in this way. I used to begin about a week ahead, and write out my impromptu speech and get it by heart. Then I brought it to the New England dinner printed on a piece of paper in my pocket, so that I could pass it to the reporters all cut and dried, and in order to do an impromptu speech as it should be done you have to indicate the places for pauses and hesitations. I put them all in it. And then you want the applause in the right places....

I do that kind of speech (I mean an offhand speech), and do it well, and make no mistake, in such a way to deceive the audience completely and make that audience believe it is an impromptu speech—that is art.

++++++++++

5

Mark Twain Speeches: An Undelivered Speech

The steamship St. Paul was to have been launched from Cramp's shipyard in Philadelphia on March 25, 1895. After the launching a luncheon was to have been given, at which Mr. Clemens was to make a speech. Just before the final word was given, a reporter asked Mr. Clemens for a copy of his speech to be delivered at the luncheon.

To facilitate the work of the reporter, he loaned him a typewritten copy of the speech. It happened, however, that when the blocks were knocked away the big ship refused to budge, and no amount of labor could move her an inch. She had stuck fast upon the ways. As a result, the launching was postponed for a week or two; but in the meantime Mr. Clemens had gone to Europe. Years after a reporter called on Mr. Clemens and submitted the manuscript of the speech, which was as follows:

Day after tomorrow I sail for England in a ship of this line, the *Paris*. It will be my fourteenth crossing in three years and a half. Therefore, my presence here, as you see, is quite natural, quite commercial. I am interested in ships. They interest me more now than hotels do. When a new ship is launched I feel a desire to go and see if she will be good quarters for me to live in, particularly if she belongs to this line, for it is by this line that I have done most of my ferrying.

People wonder why I go so much. Well, I go partly for my health, partly to familiarize myself with the road. I have gone over the same road so many times now that I know all the whales that belong along the route, and latterly it is an embarrassment to me to meet them, for they do not look glad to see me, but annoyed, and they seem to say: "Here is this old derelict again."

Earlier in life this would have pained me and made me ashamed, but I am older now, and when I

6

am behaving myself, and doing right, I do not care for a whale's opinion about me. When we are young we generally estimate an opinion by the size of the person that holds it, but later we find that that is an uncertain rule, for we realize that there are times when a hornet's opinion disturbs us more than an emperor's.

I do not mean that I care nothing at all for a whale's opinion, for that would be going to too great a length. Of course, it is better to have the good opinion of a whale than his disapproval; but my position is that if you cannot have a whale's good opinion, except at some sacrifice of principle or personal dignity, it is better to try to live without it. That is my idea about whales.

Yes, I have gone over that same route so often that I know my way without a compass, just by the waves. I know all the large waves and a good many of the small ones. Also the sunsets. I know every sunset and where it belongs just by its color. Necessarily, then, I do not make the passage now for scenery. That is all gone by.

What I prize most is safety, and in the second place swift transit and handiness. These are best furnished, by the American line, whose watertight compartments have no passage through them; no doors to be left open, and consequently no way for water to get from one of them to another in time of collision. If you nullify the peril which collisions threaten you with, you nullify the only very serious peril which attends voyages in the great liners of our day, and makes voyaging safer than staying at home.

When the *Paris* was half-torn to pieces some years ago, enough of the Atlantic ebbed and flowed through one end of her, during her long agony, to sink the fleets of the world if distributed among them; but she floated in perfect safety, and no life was lost. In time of collision the rock of Gibraltar is not safer than the *Paris* and other great ships of this line. This seems to

7

be the only great line in the world that takes a passenger from metropolis to metropolis without the intervention of tugs and barges or bridges—takes him through without breaking bulk, so to speak.

On the English side he lands at a dock; on the dock a special train is waiting; in an hour and three-quarters he is in London. Nothing could be handier. If your journey were from a sand-pit on our side to a lighthouse on the other, you could make it quicker by other lines, but that is not the case. The journey is from the city of New York to the city of London, and no line can do that journey quicker than this one, nor anywhere near as conveniently and handily. And when the passenger lands on our side he lands on the American side of the river, not in the provinces. As a very learned man said on the last voyage (he is head quartermaster of the New York land garboard streak of the middle watch),

"When we land a passenger on the American side there's nothing betwix him and his hotel but hell and the hackman."

I am glad, with you and the nation, to welcome the new ship. She is another pride, another consolation, for a great country whose mighty fleets have all vanished, and which has almost forgotten what it is to fly its flag to sea. I am not sure as to which St. Paul she is named for. Some think it is the one that is on the upper Mississippi, but the head quartermaster told me it was the one that killed Goliath. But it is not important. No matter which it is, let us give her hearty welcome and God speed.

++++++++++

My Mark Twain: William Dean Howells

He had jubilantly accepted our invitation, and had promised a speech, which it appeared afterward he had prepared with unusual care and confidence. It was his custom always to think out his speeches, mentally wording them, and then memorizing them by a peculiar system of mnemonics which he had invented. On the dinner-table a certain succession of knife, spoon, salt-cellar, and butter-plate symbolized a train of ideas, and on the billiard-table a ball, a cue, and a piece of chalk served the same purpose. With a diagram of these printed on the brain he had full command of the phrases which his excogitation had attached to them, and which embodied the ideas in perfect form.

+++++++++ +++++++++ +++++++++

9

LESSONS: Message and Speech Preparation

LESSON I: There is no substitute for preparation, rehearsal and practice

Example I:
Sir John Colville, Private Secretary to British Prime Minister Winston Churchill during the dark days of World War II said the great statesman invested "approximately one hour of preparation for every minute of delivery." This would suggest that the British Prime Minister devoted as much as thirty hours to crafting and honing speeches that lifted the hearts and spirits of a desperately besieged Britain.

Example II:
"I have a dream this afternoon that my four little children… will be judged on the basis of the content of their character, not the color of their skin."

As a speech enthusiast, you probably recognize the words of Dr. Martin Luther King and assume they are from his August 28th 1963 speech at the Lincoln Memorial in Washington, D.C.

You may be surprised to know that Dr. King's next words were, "I have a dream this afternoon that one day right here in DETROIT."

The excerpts quoted are from a powerful speech given by King at Cobo Hall, Detroit, June 23 1963, almost ten weeks before his memorable oration in Washington. King had used the "I have a dream" concept on numerous occasions prior to Washington. Indeed, one of his closest confidantes, Reverend Wyatt T. Walker advised against using the mantra in Washington as he believed it was "trite" and over-used. Thus, when Martin Luther King stepped to the microphone on that famous day with a speech text prepared by Walker, Andrew (later Ambassador) Young, Walter

Fauntleroy and Clarence B. Jones, there was NO reference to "I have a dream." However, as he moved through what was a relatively well received speech, the great Gospel singer, Mahalia Jackson shouted to him "Tell them about the dream, Martin. Tell them about the dream." The rest is history!

King departed from his text but he was not unprepared. Not only had he practiced the "dream" but he had also presented it on numerous occasions, including just one week previous in Chicago.

Winston Churchill and Dr. King had a similar mindset to Mark Twain. They practiced and prepared, prepared and practiced. It is well-nigh impossible to craft and present a wonderful speech without substantial effort, rehearsal, re-writing and more rehearsal. Let's face it, if the greats do it ....!

LESSON II: To get an audience to "believe it is an impromptu speech—that is an art."

Toastmasters World Champion of Public Speaking Darren LaCroix has a mantra that will surely be engraved on his headstone – Stagetime. Stagetime. Stagetime. As many accomplished speakers know, you will become a better and more comfortable and natural speaker, the more you practice. Twain tended to practice in isolation, but you will benefit more if you can do it in front of an audience.

Twain's contention that presenting a rehearsed speech as an impromptu one "is an art" could hardly be more accurate. "Art" to this author suggests a lack of stricture and a sense of freedom. A good speech has a sense of freedom and rhythm and flow which paradoxically requires structure, hard work and rehearsal. I am not suggesting you learn your speech by rote. What I do suggest though is that you know the flow of your speech, your points or stories are logical ordered and there is also a clear and natural logic to your transitions.

LESSON III: **Practice your material in front of smaller audiences**

In his wonderful autobiography *Life*, Keith Richards recalls that in their early years, the Rolling Stones often played to audiences of twenty-five to forty people. Playing to audiences that size allowed the Stones to hone and perfect their material.

Honing and perfecting your material in front of smaller audiences isn't just for the novice. Days before she died, Joan Rivers tested new material at a small New York comedy club, something she regularly did when not on the road. This is a practice that numerous successful comics adopt to ensure their material works before they get on the big stage.

For an enlightening perspective of how comics develop and craft their material, watch the Jerry Seinfeld documentary *Comedian*. After opting out of his TV show, Seinfeld decided to go back on the road. The documentary follows him over the year as he develops sufficient quality material for a stand up tour. After four months of consistent work, he had only twenty minutes of material. This from a man who writes material every day.

Viewing the documentary, you will also appreciate that "no man is an island" and that even the greats need support, advice and encouragement, as do you in developing your speech craft.

While this is a book about speechmaking, you will not go wrong by studying comics whose performance and audience reaction is strongly determined by the level of practice and rehearsal they put in.

++++++++++ ++++++++++ ++++++++++

How I Implement all that Learnin'!

Message and Speech Preparation

As you will see when you read chapter IV,"K – Know your Objective," I make diligent efforts to clarify my speech objective. Assuming I have done that, let's look at how I prepare one of my most popular key-notes—*The Gift of GAB* (**G**oals, **A**ttitude, **B**ehavior)—for a presentation to three different audiences.

Client I is in the Widget business and requests a keynote on *Creating a Top o' the Morning Customer Experience through The Gift of GAB*. Client II is in the healthcare arena and want a program on *Creating a Great Work Environment through The Gift of GAB*. Client III, a major consulting firm wants *Leadership through Goals, Attitude, Behavior.*

While I will present the core framework of GAB to all clients, each speech will be customized to their industry and needs.

My basic routine is to prepare an individual file for each client on my iPhone and jot down ideas, thoughts, learnings as I think of them. I check the various anecdotes and jokes that are in another file (or in my not very good memory) and consider which are appropriate or can be adapted to the respective clients. Specific Techniques include:

Google Alerts

For each client, Google Alerts are set up related not just to the particular client, but also competitors.

Social Media

Clients and competitors are followed on Twitter, Facebook, LinkedIn (and God knows what other major social media platform is hot by the time you read this!)

Industry Publications and websites

Either through client briefing or Google search, I will determine (and then follow) who are the opinion formers and major commentators in the industry.

13

Tracking your client, competitors and industry via social media—especially Twitter—is a no-brainer and will provide superb knowledge for you.

Once all this information is complete, I will have good insight into the respective industry and what the key metrics are for my widget client. Google searches like "Key challenges facing Widget industry," and "Customer Service Surveys Widget Industry" will provide a raft of knowledge for me to play back.

For the healthcare client, Google searches might be "Trends in healthcare," and "Best Healthcare Companies." Leadership searches might be "Leadership advice from Lincoln, Jack Welch, Drucker."

Note, I am already well versed in these areas having presented to hundreds of clients, but here I am searching for relevant material to connect with and educate my audience.

Rehearsing

I take the material and then write a basic outline on paper. One of the great advantages to being a professional speaker and Emcee, is that you can work while working out! Unfortunately, my poor abused body does not allow me run anymore, but I do walk a lot ensuring I get many funny looks while on the treadmill from fellow gym members who wonder "What is the Irish guy doing, talking to himself and gesticulating wildly??"

Well, by now, most of them know that "this guy" is a professional speaker rehearsing his material. I am happily surprised at the nuggets that pop out during rehearsal, nuggets that would not pop without rehearsal.

++++++++++ ++++++++++ ++++++++++

CHAPTER II

A - Audience

The country audience is the difficult audience; a passage which it will approve with a ripple will bring a crash in the city. A fair success in the country means a triumph in the city.

Mark Twain - A Biography: Albert Bigelow Paine

II

What Mark Twain Learned me 'bout understanding your **Audience**

♦ Research and KNOW your audience and its potential reaction

♦ The Law of Speaker Physics

♦ Don't be too clever

♦ Don't be offensive

♦ Give your audience permission to laugh.

♦ Different audiences react differently to material

♦ Sometimes you can be too smart and believe too much in your own brilliance!

The bulk of this chapter relates to a famous Twain speech that—despite his usual significant preparation—was perceived by many to be offensive and ill-judged.

However the manner in which he quoted material from the revered audience members he roasts—Henry Wadsworth Longfellow, Ralph Waldo Emerson and Oliver Wendell Holmes—is the work of genius. A genius who in this case misread his audience.

Twain failed to appreciate the pedestal these learned men were placed on by the audience. His (intended to be humorous) comments about the trio were roundly criticized by the press as inappropriate, something which even in later years, he failed to accept.

In a sense, the audience did not feel comfortable, or felt it appropriate to laugh at these august figures.

The lesson is that if you intend to roast someone in your audience, let that person know, so they can laugh (even if uncomfortably) and thus allow the rest of the room to join in the joke. In the words of his biographer Paine, Twain *"stepped out to meet the rainbow and got struck by lightning."*

++++++++++ ++++++++++ ++++++++++

The Story of a Speech

"An address delivered in 1877, and a review of it twenty-nine years later. The original speech was delivered at a dinner given by the publishers of The Atlantic Monthly in honor of the seventieth anniversary of the birth of John Greenleaf Whittier, at the Hotel Brunswick, Boston, December 17, 1877."

This is an occasion peculiarly meet for the digging up of pleasant reminiscences concerning literary folk; therefore I will drop lightly into history myself. Standing here on the shore of the Atlantic and contemplating certain of its largest literary billows, I am reminded of a thing which happened to me thirteen years ago, when I had just succeeded in stirring up a little Nevadian literary puddle myself, whose spume-flakes were beginning to blow thinly Californiaward. I started an inspection tramp through the southern mines of California. I was callow and conceited, and I resolved to try the virtue of my 'nom de guerre'.

I very soon had an opportunity. I knocked at a miner's lonely log cabin in the foothills of the Sierras just at nightfall. It was snowing at the time. A jaded, melancholy man of fifty, barefooted, opened the door to me. When he heard my 'nom de guerre' he looked more dejected than before. He let me in—pretty reluctantly, I thought—and after the customary bacon and beans, black coffee and hot whiskey, I took a pipe. This sorrowful man had not said three words up to this time. Now he spoke up and said, in the voice of one who is secretly suffering, "You're the fourth—I'm going to move." "The fourth what?" said I. "The fourth littery man that has been here in twenty-four hours—I'm going to move." "You don't tell me!" said I; "who were the others?" "Mr. Longfellow, Mr. Emerson, and Mr. Oliver Wendell Holmes—consound the lot!"

You can easily believe I was interested. I supplicated—three hot whiskeys did the rest—and finally the melancholy miner began. Said he:

"They came here just at dark yesterday evening, and I let them in of course. Said they were going to the Yosemite. They were a rough lot, but that's nothing; everybody looks rough that travels afoot. Mr. Emerson was a seedy little bit of a chap, red-headed. Mr. Holmes was as fat as a balloon; he weighed as much as three hundred, and had double chins all the way down to his stomach. Mr. Longfellow was built like a prize-fighter. His head was cropped and bristly, like as if he had a wig made of hair-brushes. His nose lay straight down his face, like a finger with the end joint tilted up. They had been drinking, I could see that. And what queer talk they used! Mr. Holmes inspected this cabin, then he took me by the button-hole, and says he:

> *"'Through the deep caves of thought*
> *I hear a voice that sings,*
> *Build thee more stately mansions,*
> *O my soul!'*

"Says I, 'I can't afford it, Mr. Holmes, and moreover I don't want to.' Blamed if I liked it pretty well, either, coming from a stranger, that way. However, I started to get out my bacon and beans, when Mr. Emerson came and looked on awhile, and then he takes me aside by the buttonhole and says:

> *"'Give me agates for my meat;*
> *Give me cantharids to eat;*
> *From air and ocean bring me foods,*
> *From all zones and altitudes.'*

"Says I, 'Mr. Emerson, if you'll excuse me, this ain't no hotel.' You see it sort of riled me—I warn't used to the ways of littery swells. But I went on a-sweating over my work, and next comes Mr. Longfellow and buttonholes me, and interrupts me. Says he:

> *"'Honor be to Mudjekeewis!*
> *You shall hear how Pau-Puk-Keewis—'*

"But I broke in, and says I, 'Beg your pardon, Mr. Longfellow, if you'll be so kind as to hold your yawp for about five minutes and let me get this grub ready, you'll do me proud.' Well, sir, after they'd filled up I set out the jug. Mr. Holmes looks at it, and then he fires up all of a sudden and yells:

> *"Flash out a stream of blood-red wine!*

For I would drink to other days.'

"By George, I was getting kind of worked up. I don't deny it, I was getting kind of worked up. I turns to Mr. Holmes, and says I, 'Looky here, my fat friend, I'm a-running this shanty, and if the court knows herself, you'll take whiskey straight or you'll go dry.' Them's the very words I said to him. Now I don't want to sass such famous littery people, but you see they kind of forced me. There ain't nothing onreasonable 'bout me; I don't mind a passel of guests a-treadin' on my tail three or four times, but when it comes to standing on it it's different, 'and if the court knows herself,' I says, 'you'll take whiskey straight or you'll go dry.' Well, between drinks they'd swell around the cabin and strike attitudes and spout; and pretty soon they got out a greasy old deck and went to playing euchre at ten cents a corner—on trust. I began to notice some pretty suspicious things. Mr. Emerson dealt, looked at his hand, shook his head, says:

"'I am the doubter and the doubt—'

and ca'mly bunched the hands and went to shuffling for a new layout. Says he:

> *"'They reckon ill who leave me out;*
> *They know not well the subtle ways I keep.*
> *I pass and deal again!'*

Hang'd if he didn't go ahead and do it, too! Oh, he was a cool one! Well, in about a minute things were running pretty tight, but all of a sudden I see by Mr. Emerson's eye he judged he had 'em. He had already corralled two tricks, and each of the others one. So now he kind of lifts a little in his chair and says:

> *"'I tire of globes and aces!*
> *Too long the game is played!'*

—and down he fetched a right bower. Mr. Longfellow smiles as sweet as pie and says:
"'Thanks, thanks to thee, my worthy friend,

For the lesson thou hast taught,'

—and blamed if he didn't down with another right bower! Emerson claps his hand on his bowie, Longfellow claps his on his revolver, and I went under a bunk. There was going to be trouble; but that monstrous Holmes rose up, wobbling his double chins, and says he, 'Order, gentlemen; the first man that draws, I'll lay down on him and smother him!' All quiet on the Potomac, you bet!

"They were pretty how-come-you-so by now, and they be-gun to blow. Emerson says, 'The nobbiest thing I ever wrote was "Barbara Frietchie."' Says Longfellow, 'It don't begin with my "Biglow Papers."' Says Holmes, 'My "Thanatopsis" lays over 'em both.' They mighty near ended in a fight. Then they wished they had some more company—and Mr. Emerson pointed to me and says:

> *"Is yonder squalid peasant all*
> *That this proud nursery could breed?'*

He was a-whetting his bowie on his boot—so I let it pass. Well, sir, next they took it into their heads that they would like some music; so they made me stand up and sing "When Johnny Comes Marching Home" till I dropped-at thirteen minutes past four this morning. That's what I've been through, my friend. When I woke at seven, they were leaving, thank goodness, and Mr. Longfellow had my only boots on, and his'n under his arm. Says I, 'Hold on, there, Evangeline, what are you going to do with them?' He says, 'Going to make tracks with 'em; because:

> *"Lives of great men all remind us*
> *We can make our lives sublime;*
> *And, departing, leave behind us*
> *Footprints on the sands of time.'*

"As I said, Mr. Twain, you are the fourth in twenty-four hours—and I'm going to move; I ain't suited to a littery atmos-phere."

I said to the miner, "Why, my dear sir, these were not the gracious singers to whom we and the world pay loving reverence and homage; these were impostors."

The miner investigated me with a calm eye for a while; then said he, "Ah! impostors, were they? Are you?"

I did not pursue the subject, and since then I have not travelled on my 'nom de guerre' enough to hurt. Such was the reminiscence I was moved to contribute, Mr. Chairman. In my enthusiasm I may have exaggerated the details a little, but you will easily forgive me that fault, since I believe it is the first time I have ever deflected from perpendicular fact on an occasion like this.

***January 11, 1906.* Answer to a letter received this morning:**

Dear Mrs. H.,—I am forever your debtor for reminding me of that curious passage in my life. During the first year or two after it happened, I could not bear to think of it. My pain and shame were so intense, and my sense of having been an imbecile so settled, established and confirmed, that I drove the episode entirely from my mind—and so all these twenty-eight or twenty-nine years I have lived in the conviction that my performance of that time was coarse, vulgar and destitute of humor. But your suggestion that you and your family found humor in it twenty-eight years ago moved me to look into the matter. So I commissioned a Boston typewriter to delve among the Boston papers of that bygone time and send me a copy of it................

What I have said to Mrs. H. is true. I did suffer during a year or two from the deep humiliations of that episode. But at last, in 1888, in Venice, my wife and I came across Mr. and Mrs. A. P. C., of Concord, Massachusetts, and a friendship began then of the sort which nothing but death terminates. The C.'s were very bright people and in every way charming and companionable. We were together a month or two in Venice and several months in Rome, afterwards, and one day that lamented break of mine was mentioned. And when I was on the point of lathering those people for bringing it to my mind when I had gotten the memory of it almost squelched, I perceived with joy that the C.'s were indignant about the way that my performance had been received in Boston. They poured out their opinions most freely and frankly about the frosty attitude of the people who were present at that performance, and about the Boston newspapers for the position they had taken in regard to the matter. That position was that I had been irreverent beyond belief, beyond imagination. Very well, I had accepted that as a fact for a year or two, and had been thoroughly miserable about it whenever I thought of it—which was not frequently, if I could help it.

Whenever I thought of it I wondered how I ever could have been inspired to do so unholy a thing. Well, the C.'s comforted me, but they did not persuade me to continue to think about the unhappy episode. I resisted that. I tried to get it out of my mind, and let it die, and I succeeded. Until Mrs. H.'s letter came, it had been a good twenty-five years since I had thought of that matter; and when she said that the thing was funny I wondered if possibly she might be right. At any rate, my curiosity was aroused, and I wrote to Boston and got the whole thing copied, as above set forth.

I vaguely remember some of the details of that gathering—dimly I can see a hundred people—no, perhaps fifty—shadowy figures sitting at tables feeding, ghosts now to me, and nameless forever more. I don't know who they were, but I can very distinctly see, seated at the grand table and facing the rest of us, Mr. Emerson, supernaturally grave, unsmiling; Mr. Whittier, grave, lovely, his beautiful spirit shining out of his face; Mr. Longfellow, with his silken white hair and his benignant face; Dr. Oliver Wendell Holmes, flashing smiles and affection and all good-fellowship everywhere like a rose-diamond whose facets are being turned toward the light first one way and then another—a charming man, and always fascinating, whether he was talking or whether he was sitting still (what *he* would call still, but what would be more or less motion to other people). I can see those figures with entire distinctness across this abyss of time..............

Now at that point ends all that was pleasurable about that notable celebration of Mr. Whittier's seventieth birthday—because I got up at that point and followed (the previous speaker), with what I have no doubt I supposed would be the gem of the evening—the gay oration above quoted from the Boston paper. I had written it all out the day before and had perfectly memorized it, and I stood up there at my genial and happy and self-satisfied ease, and began to deliver it. Those majestic guests, that row of venerable and still active volcanoes, listened, as did everybody else in the house, with attentive interest. Well, I delivered myself of—we'll say the first two hundred words of my speech. I was expecting no returns from that part of the speech, but this was not the case as regarded the rest of it. I arrived now at the dialogue: 'The old miner said, "You are the fourth, I'm going to move." "The fourth what?" said I. He answered, "The fourth littery man that has been here in twenty-four hours. I am going to move." "Why, you don't tell me," said I. "Who were the others?" "Mr. Longfellow, Mr. Emerson, Mr. Oliver Wendell Holmes, consound the lot—"'

Now then the house's *attention* continued, but the expression of interest in the faces turned to a sort of black frost. I wondered what the trouble was. I didn't know. I went on, but with difficulty—I struggled along, and entered upon that miner's fearful description of the bogus Emerson, the bogus Holmes, the bogus Longfellow, always hoping—but with a gradually perishing hope—that somebody would laugh, or that somebody would at least smile, but nobody did. I didn't know enough to give it up and sit down, I was too new to public speaking, and so I went on with this awful performance, and carried it clear through to the end, in front of a body of people who seemed turned to stone with horror. It was the sort of expression their faces would have worn if I had been making these remarks about the Deity and the rest of the Trinity; there is no milder way in which to describe the petrified condition and the ghastly expression of those people.

When I sat down it was with a heart which had long ceased to beat. I shall never be as dead again as I was then. I shall never be as miserable again as I was then. I speak now as one who doesn't know what the condition of things may be in the next world, but in this one I shall never be as wretched again as I was then. Howells, who was near me, tried to say a comforting word, but couldn't get beyond a gasp. There was no use—he understood the whole size of the disaster. He had good intentions, but the words froze before they could get out. It was an atmosphere that would freeze anything. If Benvenuto Cellini's salamander had been in that place he would not have survived to be put into Cellini's autobiography.

There was a frightful pause. There was an awful silence, a desolating silence. Then the next man on the list had to get up—there was no help for it. That was Bishop—Bishop had just burst handsomely upon the world with a most acceptable novel, which had appeared in the "Atlantic Monthly," a place which would make any novel respectable and any author noteworthy. In this case the novel itself was recognized as being, without extraneous help, respectable.

Bishop was away up in the public favor, and he was an object of high interest, consequently there was a sort of national expectancy in the air; we may say our American millions were standing, from Maine to Texas and from Alaska to Florida, holding their breath, their lips parted, their hands ready to applaud when Bishop should get up on that occasion, and for the first time in his life speak in public. It was under these damaging conditions that he got up to "make good," as the vulgar say. I had spoken several times before, and that is the reason why I was able to go on without dying in my tracks, as I ought to have done—but Bishop had had no experience. He was up facing those awful deities—facing those other people, those strangers—facing human beings for the first time in his life, with a speech to utter. No doubt it was well packed away in his memory, no doubt it was fresh and usable, until I had been heard from. I suppose that after that, and under the smothering pall of that dreary silence, it began to waste away and disappear out of his head like the rags breaking from the edge of a fog, and presently there wasn't any fog left. He didn't go on—he didn't last long. It was not many sentences after his first before he began to hesitate, and break, and lose his grip, and totter, and wobble, and at last he slumped down in a limp and mushy pile.

Well, the program for the occasion was probably not more than one-third finished, but it ended there. Nobody rose. The next man hadn't strength enough to get up, and everybody looked so dazed, so stupefied, paralyzed, it was impossible for anybody to do anything, or even try. Nothing could go on in that strange atmosphere. Howells mournfully, and without words, hitched himself to Bishop and me and supported us out of the room. It was very kind—he was most generous.

He towed us tottering away into some room in that building, and we sat down there. I don't know what my remark was now, but I know the nature of it. It was the kind of remark you make when you know that nothing in the world can help your case. But Howells was honest—he had to say the heart-breaking things he did say: that there was no help for this calamity, this shipwreck, this cataclysm; that this was the most disastrous thing that had ever happened in anybody's history—and then he added, "That is, for *you*—and consider what you have done for Bishop. It is bad enough in your case, you deserve to suffer. You have committed this crime, and you deserve to have all you are going to get. But here is an innocent man. Bishop had never done you any harm, and see what you have done to him. He can never hold his head up again. The world can never look upon Bishop as being a live person. He is a corpse."

That is the history of that episode of twenty-eight years ago, which pretty nearly killed me with shame during that first year or two whenever it forced its way into my mind.

Now, then, I take that speech up and examine it. As I said, it arrived this morning, from Boston. I have read it twice, and unless I am an idiot, it hasn't a single defect in it from the first word to the last. It is just as good as good can be. It is smart; it is saturated with humor. There isn't a suggestion of coarseness or vulgarity in it anywhere. What could have been the matter with that house? It is amazing, it is incredible, that they didn't shout with laughter, and those deities the loudest of them all. Could the fault have been with me? Did I lose courage when I saw those great men up there whom I was going to describe in such a strange fashion? If that happened, if I showed doubt, that can account for it, for you can't be successfully funny if you show that you are afraid of it. Well, I can't account for it, but if I had those beloved and revered old literary immortals back here now on the platform at Carnegie Hall I would take that same old speech, deliver it, word for word, and melt them till they'd run all over that stage. Oh, the fault must have been with *me*, it is not in the speech at all.

++++++++++

New York World Interview, November 20 1884

Audiences have their peculiarities, you know. It is a great inspiration to find a particular individual fairly respond to you as if you were in telegraphic communication with him. You are tempted to address yourself solely to him. I've tried that experiment. Sometimes it is dangerous. Laughter is very infectious, and when you see a man give one big guffaw you begin to laugh with him in spite of yourself. Now, it will not do for the lecturer to laugh. His is a grave and serious business however it might strike the audience. His demeanor should be grave and serious. He should not even smile.

++++++++++

Letter fragment, 1891

And I was a lecturer on the public platform a number of seasons and was a responder to toasts at all the different kinds of banquets—and so I know a great many secrets about audiences—secrets not to be got out of books, but only acquirable by experience.

++++++++++ ++++++++++ ++++++++++

LESSONS: Audience

LESSON I: Research and KNOW your audience and its potential reaction

If the great Mark Twain bombed, even after studious preparation of a speech, you can be reasonably sure that at some stage you are likely to suffer that uncomfortable cold sweat at the back of your neck as you wonder why the audience is not paying attention or appreciating your wit and wisdom.

Jay Leno says "Everyone bombs" and indeed he quite likely felt some of that cold sweat when presenting at the 2010 White House Correspondents Dinner. "Jay Leno BOMBS at White House Dinner" screamed the Huffington Post.

For you as a speaker, it is critical to have a good appreciation of who is in the audience, what their expectations are and why they are there.

Twain's disastrous Whittier speech was in many ways genuinely funny and demonstrated substantial research. However, the audience would not have expected to see three great men of American literature "roasted" in a manner that at times was perceived as insulting – "Mr. Emerson was a seedy little bit of a chap, red-headed. Mr. Holmes was as fat as a balloon; he weighed as much as three hundred, and had double chins all the way down to his stomach." That type of comment is likely to make many wince if the target is in the room. Almost certainly had the trio not been there, Twain's comments would have evoked substantial laughter.

Comic Steven Colbert suffered a similar fate at the 2006 Correspondents Dinner where he savaged George W. Bush and his Iraq policy. As a very successful, politically aware comic, Colbert probably lost little sleep that a sometime partisan audience didn't appreciate his humor.

Now that we have established that even the great speakers and performers sometimes get it wrong, how can we ensure that you do not suffer a similar fate?

In most cases, it should be easy to determine who will be in the audience and what they are expecting from the speaker.

Consult with the event planner for advice. Determine what are the challenges and worries that are keeping audience members awake at night. Ask for a final brief a few days before the event and it is particularly important to be aware of any negative situations or events that may have happened since you were first briefed.

LESSON II: The Law of Speaker Physics

Twain knew "a great many secrets about audiences - secrets not to be got out of books, but only acquirable by experience."

One concept that presenters do not pay sufficient attention to is what I refer to as **The Law of Speaker Physics** which goes as follows:

The more open space there is in a room, the less energy there is in the room.

The less open space there is in a room, the more energy there is in the room.

There is a reason why comedy clubs seat patrons close to each other even if the house is almost empty. Laughter is infectious as is personal energy.

If you can influence the seating arrangements for your speech, remember The Law of Speaker Physics. In practice this should mean that if you expect seventy one people to attend your event, set the room for seventy one seats! If you are speaking in a large auditorium that you expect will be only half full, ask the event planner to cordon off a large section to ensure that you are speaking to a "packed house."

LESSON III: Don't Be Too Clever or Offensive

I know, I know! You are saying "Wow, tell me something I don't know."

Well, Mark Twain the finest and most popular speaker of his generation, goofed and stepped over the line with his Whittier Birthday Speech. The *Cincinnati Commercial* excoriated him for his "bad taste" and continued "It is assumed that he ought to have known better; that even with his innocent desire to enliven the proceedings with something humorously quaint, and mix it with quotations from the respective writings of the poets, the instincts of a gentleman would have forbidden its presentation in a character-sketch so coarse and absurd in every incident. It will require a good deal of ingenuity on the part of the humorist to extricate himself gracefully from the predicament in which he is involved, and soften away the painful sensations that followed his unique performance."

Off stage, Twain was quite a profane individual - "If I cannot swear in heaven I shall not stay there," and while some of his lesser known material is—shall we say—blue!, he rarely again shocked his audience with his material.

There is one simple, oft-repeated rule when it comes to offensive material – If in doubt, leave it out.

LESSON IV: Give your Audience Permission to Laugh

At the Whittier speech, Twain's audience was not expecting a roast of Holmes, Longfellow and Emerson. It seems also that the celebrated trio were held in such high esteem that it was not expected nor accepted that you make fun of them. (Oh, how times have changed!)

Although Twain was later assured by Longfellow and Holmes that they had not taken any offence (Emerson was in the early stages of senility), it seems that they did not obviously laugh at his material on the night. Had they done so, the audience would have followed. The key point here is that if you are going to roast someone, make sure the person being roasted is aware of the fate that is about to befall them!. In laughing (however uncomfortably) at his roast, he is giving his fellow audience member permission to laugh.

Another simple, but very important practice is - if you want your audience to laugh: do not step on their laughter. When you say something funny, pause, let the humor filter to their brain (which does take time) and give them time to laugh. When your audience has laughed once, they will laugh easier the next time and the more your audience laughs, the more you will make that vital connection.

Quite often, you will be surprised at what your audience finds humorous, but this is just one more advantage of rehearsing and practicing in front of smaller groups before you have to make that vital speech.

LESSON V: Different Audiences React Differently to Material

Novice speakers sometimes wonder why the wonderful quip that had audiences rolling in the aisles last week evoked zero reaction at the next event. Remember Twain said "A fair success in the country means a triumph in the city."

Experienced speakers understand that the reception can be impacted by a number of elements. As a speaker to associations and corporations on a range of topics to improve people, performance and productivity enjoyably, I pay particular attention to factors that will impact the reception of my message.

The time of your presentation impacts reception. For instance!

- First thing in the morning, the audience has not woken up!
- Just before lunch, you are the only person keeping them from their food.
- Then you have the "Graveyard shift", immediately after lunch when your audience is drowsy
- As final speaker, well, now you are delaying them from getting out in front of the rush hour traffic!

OK, those examples may be slightly facetious, but there is also some truth to them. Apparently simple things can impact reaction. For instance a sales team may react quite differently and became extremely reserved when senior management enters the room.

Once you understand that each audience has its own personality, experience will tell you what to expect. There will be times when that magic connection does not happen, but the more you get out "into the arena," the less likely you are to feel that cold sweat at the back of the neck! And if you do, remember experience is a wonderful teacher.

++++++++++ ++++++++++ ++++++++++

How I Implement all that Learnin'!

Audience

It is a genuine wonder to me how the reception of exactly the same keynote can vary depending on the time of day, the location, audience size, audience sex, distance from audience, room size, room height, room temperature, room acoustics, seating arrangements, company mood, CEO mood and personality (oh, yes!), in-house or external meeting, and if there is breaking news story or a big sports game, well, you might as well accept the smartphones will be coming out. And you thought it was all down to the speech!

I have a series of very basic questions I ask my client at the outset. These include

Who is the audience?

Reason for meeting?

How many?

Age group?

Sex?

Length of tenure?

Mood / Morale?

Interesting personal anecdotes

Can I tell those interesting personal anecdotes?

Entertainment the previous evening? (Oh, the stories I could tell!)

You may think that all of the above is basic commonsense. Of course, but we both know that commonsense is not really all that common. Meeting planners can provide horror stories as to how speakers have misread or offended their audience. Those speakers did not get invited back, and in an industry that has a vibrant communication culture, you can be sure the word spreads. At a recent convention I spoke at in my wonderful Ireland, a fellow speaker referred to Ireland as part of the United Kingdom. Now if there is one thing to get someone from the Republic of Ireland agitated, it is being told he is part of the UK. A number of audience members heckled him (to be fair rather good-humoredly), but he had lost credibility and connection with the audience. Why? He had not done basic homework.

Room Layout

When relatively new to the professional speaking business, I presented at a large convention hall in the southern states. I was the closing speaker of a three day conference. As you might imagine, a number of delegates had already hit the road. So we now had about 1,500 people in a convention hall set up for 2,500, a convention hall that could hold up to 4,000! Most of those 1,500 sat at the back of the convention hall, a convention hall with very tall ceilings! Thankfully, the organizers had large screens on either side of the stage so I was not a speck on the horizon. However, when I went on stage to speak, my first impression was the enormous space between me and the audience. The presentation went very well and I received excellent reviews, but the mistake I made (I probably lacked the confidence to do it at the time) was I should have come off the stage and walked to the audience to reduce the open space between me and the audience. (In my early years, I had not fully appreciated that something as basic as a wide open space IS a barrier between you and the audience. Had I come off stage, the cameras would have picked me up and projected my Irish mug on the screens.

Today, when I have the opportunity to influence the room layout, I encourage the planner to keep the seating compact but not too tight; ask for a slightly higher room temperature if it is primarily a female audience; no U-shaped room if a training session and no views of the swimming pool! And I reference the Law of Speaker Physics to my planner:

The more open space there is in a room, the less energy there is in the room.
The less open space there is in a room, the more energy there is in the room.

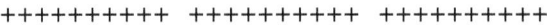

CHAPTER III

R - Relate to your Audience

It seems as if I must have been insane when I wrote that speech and saw no harm in it.

Mark Twain Letter to W. D. Howells

III

What Mark Twain Learned me 'bout how to **Relate to your Audience**

- ◆ Work the room before your speech
- ◆ A well written introduction, properly delivered, sets the scene for the speaker
- ◆ Customize your speech
- ◆ Your audience has experienced the same emotions, the highs and lows that you have. Share your experience
- ◆ Use evocative material and anecdotes
- ◆ Experience is the best and hardest taskmaster

+++++++++ ++++++++++ ++++++++++

Mark Twain's Speeches: Compliments and Degrees

Now here is a gold-miner's compliment. It is forty-two years old. It was my introduction to an audience to which I lectured in a log school-house. There were no ladies there. I wasn't famous then. They didn't know me. Only the miners were there, with their breeches tucked into their boot tops and with clay all over them. They wanted someone to introduce me, and they selected a miner, who protested, saying:

"I don't know anything about this man. Anyhow, I only know two things about him. One is, he has never been in jail, and the other is, I don't know why."

++++++++++

Mark Twain – A Biography: Albert Bigelow Paine

At all places visited by lecturers there was a committee, and it was the place of the chairman to introduce the lecturer, a privilege which he valued, because it gave him a momentary association with distinction and fame. Clemens was a great

37

disappointment to these officials. He had learned long ago that he could introduce himself more effectively than anyone else. His usual formula was to present himself as the chairman of the committee, introducing the lecturer of the evening; then, with what was in effect a complete change of personality, to begin his lecture. It was always startling and amusing, always a success; but the papers finally printed this formula, which took the freshness out of it, so that he had to invent others. Sometimes he got up with the frank statement that he was introducing himself because he had never met anyone who could pay a proper tribute to his talents.

++++++++++

Adventures of Huckleberry Finn

And then when I went up to bed she come up with me and fetched her candle, and tucked me in, and mothered me so good I felt mean, and like I couldn't look her in the face; and she set down on the bed and talked with me a long time, and said what a splendid boy he was, and didn't seem to want to ever stop talking about him; and kept asking me every now and then if I reckoned he could a got lost, or hurt, or maybe drownded, and might be laying at this minute somewheres suffering or dead, and she not by him to help him, and so the tears would drip down silent, and I would tell her that Sid was all right, and would be home in the morning, sure; and she would squeeze my hand, or maybe kiss me, and tell me to say it again, and keep on saying it, because it done her good, and she was in so much trouble. And when she was going away she looked down in my eyes so steady and gentle, and says:

"The door ain't going to be locked, and there's the window and the rod; but you'll be good, WON'T you? And you won't go? For MY sake."

Laws knows I WANTED to go bad enough to see about Tom, and was all intending to go; but after that I wouldn't a went, not for kingdoms.

But she was on my mind and Tom was on my mind, so I slept very restless. And twice I went down the rod away in the night, and slipped around front, and see her setting there by her candle in the window with her eyes towards the road and the tears in them; and I wished I could do something for her, but I couldn't, only to swear that I wouldn't never do nothing to grieve her any more. And the third time I waked up at dawn, and slid down, and she was there yet, and her candle was most out, and her old gray head was resting on her hand, and she was asleep.

++++++++++

Mark Twain Speeches: The Babies (where Twain toasted General Ulysses S. Grant at a dinner hosted by his former colleagues – Chicago, November 1879)

I like that. We have not all had the good fortune to be ladies. We have not all been generals, or poets, or statesmen; but when the toast works down to the babies, we stand on common ground. It is a shame that for a thousand years the world's banquets have utterly ignored the baby, as if he didn't amount to anything. If you will stop and think a minute—if you will go back fifty or one hundred years to your early married life and recontemplate your first baby—you will remember that he amounted to a good deal, and even something over.

You soldiers all know that when that little fellow arrived at family headquarters you had to hand in your resignation. He took entire command. You became his lackey, his mere body-servant, and you had to stand around too. He was not a commander who made allowances for time, distance, weather, or anything else. You had to execute his order whether it was possible or not. And there was only one form of marching in his manual of tactics, and that was the double-quick. He treated you with every sort of insolence and disrespect, and the bravest of you didn't dare to say a word. You could face the death-storm at Donelson and Vicksburg, and give back blow for blow; but when he clawed your whiskers, and pulled your hair, and twisted your nose, you had to take it.

When the thunders of war were sounding in your ears you set your faces toward the batteries, and advanced with steady tread; but when he turned on the terrors of his war whoop you advanced in the other direction, and mighty glad of the chance, too. When he called for soothing-syrup, did you venture to throw out any side-remarks about certain services being unbecoming an officer and a gentleman? No. You got up and got it.

When he ordered his pap bottle and it was not warm, did you talk back? Not you. You went to work and warmed it. You even descended so far in your menial office as to take a suck at that warm, insipid stuff yourself, to see if it was right—three parts water to one of milk, a touch of sugar to modify the colic, and a drop of peppermint to kill those immortal hiccoughs. I can taste that stuff yet. And how many things you learned as you went along!

Sentimental young folks still take stock in that beautiful old saying that when the baby smiles in his sleep, it is because the angels are whispering to him. Very pretty, but too thin—simply wind on the stomach, my friends. If the baby proposed to take a walk at his usual hour, two o'clock in the morning, didn't you rise up promptly and remark, with a mental addition which would not improve a Sunday-school book much, that that was the very thing you were about to propose yourself?

++++++++++

Mark Twain Notebook

Only he who has seen better days and lives to see better days again knows their full value.

++++++++++

Mark Twain: Archibald Henderson

His speech introducing General Hawley of Connecticut to a Republican meeting at Elmira, New York, is an admirable example of his laconic art: "General Hawley is a member of my church at Hartford, and the author of 'Beautiful Snow.' Maybe he will deny that. But I am only here to give him a character from his last place. As a pure citizen, I respect him; as a personal friend of years, I have the warmest regard for him; as a neighbour, whose vegetable garden adjoins mine, why—why, I watch him. As the author of 'Beautiful Snow,' he has added a new pang to winter. He is a square, true man in honest politics, and I must say he occupies a mighty lonesome position. So broad, so bountiful is his character that he never turned a tramp empty-handed from his door, but always gave him a letter of introduction to me. Pure, honest, incorruptible, that is Joe Hawley. Such a man in politics is like a bottle of perfumery in a glue factory—it may modify the stench, but it doesn't destroy it. I haven't said any more of him than I would say of myself. Ladies and gentlemen, this is General Hawley."

++++++++++

Mark Twain's Speeches: Sixty–Seventh Birthday

I went out there last June, and I met in that town of Hannibal a schoolmate of mine, John Briggs, whom I had not seen for more than fifty years. I tell you, that was a meeting! That pal whom I had known as a little boy long ago, and knew now as a stately man three or four inches over six feet and browned by exposure to many climes, he was back there to see that old place again. We spent a whole afternoon going about here and there and yonder, and hunting up the scenes and talking of the crimes which we had committed so long ago.

It was a heartbreaking delight, full of pathos, laughter, and tears, all mixed together; and we called the roll of the boys and girls that we picnicked and sweet-hearted with so many years ago, and there were hardly half a dozen of them left; the rest were in their graves; and we went up there on the summit of that hill, a treasured place in my memory, the summit of Holiday's Hill, and looked out again over that magnificent panorama of the Mississippi River, sweeping along league after league, a level green paradise on one side, and retreating capes and promontories as far as you could see on the other, fading away in the soft, rich lights of the remote distance. I recognized then that I was seeing now the most enchanting river view the planet could furnish. I never knew it when I was a boy; it took an educated eye that had travelled over the globe to know and appreciate it; and John said, "Can you point out the place where Bear Creek used to be before the railroad came?" I said, "Yes, it ran along yonder." "And can you point out the swimming-hole?" "Yes, out there." And he said, "Can you point out

41

the place where we stole the skiff?" Well, I didn't know which one he meant.

Such a wilderness of events had intervened since that day, more than fifty years ago, it took me more than five minutes to call back that little incident, and then I did call it back; it was a white skiff, and we painted it red to allay suspicion. And the saddest, saddest man came along—a stranger he was—and he looked that red skiff over so pathetically, and he said: "Well, if it weren't for the complexion I'd know whose skiff that was." He said it in that pleading way, you know, that appeals for sympathy and suggestion; we were full of sympathy for him, but we weren't in any condition to offer suggestions. I can see him yet as he turned away with that same sad look on his face and vanished out of history forever. I wonder what became of that man. I know what became of the skiff. Well, it was a beautiful life, a lovely life. There was no crime. Merely little things like pillaging orchards and watermelon-patches and breaking the Sabbath—we didn't break the Sabbath often enough to signify—once a week perhaps. But we were good boys, good Presbyterian boys, all Presbyterian boys, and loyal and all that; anyway, we were good Presbyterian boys when the weather was doubtful; when it was fair, we did wander a little from the fold.

++++++++++

From Mark Twain Letters: Arranged with comment by Albert Bigelow Paine

The (disastrous) speech was made at John Greenleaf Whittier's seventieth birthday dinner, given by the Atlantic staff on the evening of December 17, 1877. It was intended as a huge joke—a joke that would shake the sides of these venerable Boston deities, Longfellow, Emerson, Holmes, and the rest of that venerated group. Clemens had been a favorite at the *Atlantic* lunches and dinners—a speech by him always an event. This time he decided to outdo himself.

He did that, but not in the way he had intended. To use one of his own metaphors, he stepped out to meet the rainbow and got struck by lightning. His joke was not of the Boston kind or size. When its full nature burst upon the company—

when the ears of the assembled diners heard the sacred names of Longfellow, Emerson, and Holmes lightly associated with human aspects removed—oh, very far removed —from Cambridge and Concord, a chill fell upon the diners that presently became amazement, and then creeping paralysis. Nobody knew afterward whether the great speech that he had so gaily planned ever came to a natural end or not. Somebody—the next on the program—attempted to follow him, but presently the company melted out of the doors and crept away into the night. It seemed to Mark Twain that his career had come to an end. Back in Hartford, sweating and suffering through sleepless nights, he wrote Howells his anguish.

++++++++++

Letter to W. D. Howells

MY DEAR HOWELLS,—My sense of disgrace does not abate. It grows. I see that it is going to add itself to my list of permanencies—a list of humiliations that extends back to when I was seven years old, and which keep on persecuting me regardless of my repentancies.

I feel that my misfortune has injured me all over the country; therefore it will be best that I retire from before the public at present. It will hurt the *Atlantic* for me to appear in its pages, now. So it is my opinion and my wife's that the telephone story had better be suppressed. Will you return those proofs or revises to me, so that I can use the same on some future occasion?

It seems as if I must have been insane when I wrote that speech and saw no harm in it, no disrespect toward those men whom I reverenced so much. And what shame I brought upon you, after what you said in introducing me! It burns me like fire to think of it.

The whole matter is a dreadful subject—let me drop it here—at least on paper.

Penitently yrs,
MARK.

++++++++++

43

My Mark Twain: William Dean Howells (writing on Twain's disastrous performance referenced in The Story of a Speech.)

He had jubilantly accepted our invitation, and had promised a speech, which it appeared afterward he had prepared with unusual care and confidence....... He believed he had been particularly fortunate in his notion for the speech of that evening, and he had worked it out in joyous self-reliance. It was the notion of three tramps, three deadbeats, visiting a California mining-camp, and imposing themselves upon the innocent miners as respectively Ralph Waldo Emerson, Henry Wadsworth Longfellow, and Oliver Wendell Holmes. The humor of the conception must prosper or must fail according to the mood of the hearer, but Clemens felt sure of compelling this to sympathy, and he looked forward to an unparalleled triumph.

But there were two things that he had not taken into account. One was the species of religious veneration in which these men were held by those nearest them, a thing that I should not be able to realize to people remote from them in time and place. They were men of extraordinary dignity, of the thing called presence, for want of some clearer word, so that no one could well approach them in a personally light or trifling spirit.

I do not suppose that anybody more truly valued them or more piously loved them than Clemens himself, but the intoxication of his fancy carried him beyond the bounds of that regard, and emboldened him to the other thing which he had not taken into account-namely, the immense hazard of working his fancy out before their faces, and expecting them to enter into the delight of it. If neither Emerson, nor Longfellow, nor Holmes had been there, the scheme might possibly have carried, but even this is doubtful, for those who so devoutly honored them would have overcome their horror with difficulty, and perhaps would not have overcome it at all.

++++++++++ ++++++++++ ++++++++++

LESSONS: Relate to your Audience

LESSON I: Work the Room BEFORE your Speech

In many situations, your speech and your performance can (and preferably should) start before you ever get on the stage. Many successful professional speakers are not technically the most gifted speakers, but they know how to, and are excellent at, relating and connecting with their audience.

One highly effective trick to build that all important relationship with your audience is to talk with them prior to your event. I appreciate this is not always practical, but as the room or auditorium is filling, the speaker who wanders the room, welcomes audience members and gets involved in chit-chat likely will have that audience on his side and looking forward to her speech before she utters one formal word from the stage.

Twain in a sense "worked the room" before the speech with some of his pre-event publicity. Famously, for his debut in San Francisco, he created a flyer which read in part:
"A SPLENDID ORCHESTRA is in town, but has not been engaged.
MAGNIFICENT FIREWORKS were in contemplation for this occasion but the idea has been abandoned.
A GRAND TORCHLIGHT PROCESSION may be expected. In fact the public are privileged to expect what they please."

LESSON II: A Well Written Introduction Sets the Scene for the Speaker.

Twain believed a good introduction was so important that eventually he introduced himself, not trusting the respective committee chair to introduce him in an appropriate manner.

Your introduction should be concise and relevant to your audience. Many speakers treat their introduction as if it were the overture to an orchestral work. Mozart and Beethoven would not be happy for someone to interfere with their respective overtures. Similarly, if you believe (as you should) that your introduction is important in setting the scene for your speech, you should request your introduction is read as written.

One of the doyens of the professional speaker circuit, the outrageous (her term) and endearing Mikki Williams presents the event planner with an introduction featuring clear directions as to how it should be read and when and where the introducer is to pause.

LESSON III: Customize your Speech

You know the scene. The speaker is on stage telling you how wonderful you all are and how "you too can win the gold, climb the highest peak, overcome disaster, run the race, fight the good fight..... just like me!" and you know that this canned presentation was probably presented the previous week, word for word to your competitor. To be fair, the speaker did remember to change the company name! In my experience, the canned speech presented by the "flavor of the month" speaker tends to have a short (but often lucrative) shelf life.

Relating to your audience requires making a connection, empathizing, and showing you know their challenges, that you comprehend their pain and emotion.

Today, in the age of the internet, there is no excuse for not customizing your speech. Consider Mark Twain's Whittier speech for a moment. Yes, in many ways it was a disaster, but consider the amount of work and research the great humorist put in to customize the speech and insert appropriate quotes from the respective trio.

He dropped in relevant quotes from *The Chambered Nautilus* by Oliver Wendell Holmes

> "'Through the deep caves of thought
> I hear a voice that sings,
> Build thee more stately mansions,
> O my soul!

From *Brahma* by Ralph Waldo Emerson, he inserted
> "'They reckon ill who leave me out;
> They know not well the subtle ways I keep.
> I pass and deal again!'

And from *A Psalm of Life* by Longfellow came the lines
> "'Lives of great men all remind us
> We can make our lives sublime;

And, departing, leave behind us
Footprints on the sands of time.'

At a time when content like this could only be garnered by ploughing through books, that is a very significant and impressive level of customization.

One of the reasons it is important to understand who is in the audience is because it will help you properly prepare. The examples you should cite to travel agents focused on adventure travel are sure to be different to the travel agent focused on the Baby Boomer luxury segment.

LESSON IV: Your Audience has Experienced the Same Emotions, the Highs and Lows You Have.

It is highly unlikely that you or your audience will answer any of the following questions in the negative.

Have you struggled at some time in your life?

Have you had good days?

Have you had bad days?

Do you have a favorite memory?

Can you remember a time when you felt lost, alone, vulnerable?

Can you recall at least one person who influenced you?

Can you recall a time when you felt great, on top of the world?

The incidents and events that trigger those memories may be different for each member of your audience, but the emotions are not. Each of us has, like Hamlet "suffered the slings and arrows of outrageous fortune." Mark Twain understood that and provided images and experiences that his audience could relate to, even if they might not have been able to articulate them in the same manner.

++++++++++ ++++++++++ ++++++++++

How I Implement all that Learnin'!

Relate to your Audience

Following a keynote presentation, a New York client wrote:

"Conor, we want to thank you again for a wonderful presentation!!! The verbal evaluations were great!!! A hit!!! You are a natural. It was so nice how you met everyone at the tables- I never saw that before from a speaker."

Despite the fact that my client may not have seen other speakers work the room before, I am not alone in connecting with audience members prior to my engagement. Good speakers know it helps to break the ice.

My approach is to engage in light-hearted conversation that might go something like:

"We are really looking forward to hearing your presentation."

"Oh, you'll change your mind once I start. Are you sure you are in the right room?"

The result is laughter and a connection with the audience. I make a deliberate effort to go to the four corners of the room, starting from the front and working to the back. I start from the front so "everyone" sees me chatting and having some fun. Networking to the back of the room is critical, because you want all of the room to be with you as you speak. I use this format whether I am doing a humorous, motivational speech or a Leadership program to senior executives of a Fortune 500. Remember, we all experience the same emotions. People want to be connected to.

The Introduction

This is the opening paragraph of my introduction for almost every event:

"Our speaker today Conor Cunneen is an Irishman happily exiled in Chicago, where he says: The Guinness is great .... The natives are friendly and ...... He has been force-fed more corned beef and green beer than he ever had in Ireland! (PAUSE)"

I know this introduction will get laughter, the extent of which will depend on just how competent the reader is! I have pulled the Guinness reference on a few occasions where I felt there may have been an anti-alcohol bias, but whether it is to nurses, sales, marketing, leadership or computer nerds, this is generally the opening of my introduction.

I follow this up with reference to appropriate credentials for that particular audience, thus creating a level of credibility for the Irish guy who just a few minutes previous was working the room making a connection.

While I reference appropriate awards or recognition in my introduction, I do not tell my audience what a wonderful person I am! They can decide that for themselves. My average intro is about 160 words long which can take up to 90 seconds to read when allowing for audience reaction to some of my corny humor and the pauses I request. More and more, I now ask my introducer to confirm they have read my introduction a few times prior to getting on that stage. A number of my speaker colleagues, who like me, believe the introduction sets the scene for what is to come insist the introducer reads the copy to them to make sure timing, enunciation etc. is correct.

Customize

As indicated in *Chapter II – Audience*, by the time I get to the room, I will have completed a significant level of research about my client in preparation for the speech. I intersperse that knowledge into the core framework of my keynote. My objective is to have the audience thinking, "Hey, this guy knows our business." I am not presenting myself as an expert on their business, but as an expert who can help their business.

I recently presented to a Bond Insurance client. Believe me, this is a niche section of the insurance business and one I had not heard of prior to the client connecting with me. An audience member approached after my keynote and asked "Have you worked in Bond Insurance? You seem to know a lot about what makes us tick." As you can imagine, I was delighted at that response, but it happened because the homework had been done.

As part of my speech preparation, I had Googled "Bond Insurance," "Bond Insurance Publications" (that was gold!) and also a number of companies I knew would be in the audience. I also knew that sales people are the same all over the world, encountering the same general challenges whether they

49

are selling cars or are insurance producers. The homework paid dividends.

Folder

Develop a consistent process to capture your ideas and thoughts. Some speakers keep a journal or notepad. The issue I have with a written document is that you are unlikely to have it with you all the time. I have a folder on my iPhone (which my long-suffering wife swears I am glued to) titled *Customize*. I also downloaded an excellent free digital recorder—Voice Record Pro—from iTunes where I will also capture my thoughts. Here are just two examples from my Customize folder:

Example I:

When doing a "humorous motivational" program to an Optometrist conference I told them about a high school girlfriend I had.

"Her name was Iris! My friends said she wasn't right for me, but I had a kind of a blind spot for her. I remember she had an allergic reaction which caused her face to swell. The teacher said she was a dilated pupil!" Groan! OK, pure corn and hokum but they were laughing loud and hard

Example II:

Presenting to a major hardware sales conference, I started with: "The oldest hardware store in the country is Elwood Adams Hardware in Worcester, Massachusetts. When it was founded by Daniel Waldo and his son in 1782, they could hardly have envisaged an industry that today is worth ..."

Skimming through my Customize file for this section, I happened on a quote from Bruce Springsteen's sidekick, guitarist Steve Van Zandt. "We just reach for greatness all the time and we expect everybody around us to do the same."

Think about it! Relate to your Audience and you will be on the road to greatness.

++++++++++ ++++++++++ ++++++++++

CHAPTER IV

K - Know your Objective

" 'My dear Clemens, whatever you do, never sell your audience.' And that," continued Mr. Clemens, "was my first really profitable lesson."

Mark Twain: Archibald Henderson

IV

*What Mark Twain Learned me 'bout **Know your Objective***

♦ Begin with the end in mind

♦ Know what you want the audience to do, feel, think when you are finished

♦ Determine if you wish to inform, persuade, inspire, entertain or educate

++++++++++ ++++++++++ ++++++++++

Mark Twain - A Biography: Albert Bigelow Paine

At a Mark Twain memorial meeting (November 30, 1910), where the few who were left of his old companions told over quaint and tender memories, George Cable recalled their reading days together and told of Mark Twain's conscientious effort to do his best, to be worthy of himself, regardless of all other concerns. He told how when they had been traveling for a while Clemens seemed to realize that he was only giving the audience nonsense; making them laugh at trivialities which they would forget before they had left the entertainment hall.

Cable said that up to that time he had supposed Clemens's chief thought was the entertainment of the moment, and that if the audience laughed he was satisfied. He told how he had sat in the wings, waiting his turn, and heard the tides of laughter gather and roll forward and break against the footlights, time and time again, and how he had believed his colleague to be glorying in that triumph. What was his surprise, then, on the way to the hotel in the carriage, when Clemens groaned and seemed writhing in spirit and said: "Oh, Cable, I am demeaning myself. I am allowing myself to be a mere buffoon. It's ghastly. I can't endure it any longer."

Cable added that all that night and the next day Mark Twain devoted himself to the study and rehearsal of selections which were justified not only as humor, but as literature and art.

53

++++++++++
Mark Twain: Archibald Henderson

In commenting on the reasons for the broadening and deepening of his humor with the passage of time, Mr. Clemens once remarked to me: "I succeeded in the long run, where Shillaber, Doesticks, and Billings failed, because they never had an ideal higher than that of merely being funny. The first great lesson of my life was the discovery that I had to live down my past. When I first began to lecture, and in my earlier writings, my sole idea was to make comic capital out of everything I saw and heard. My object was not to tell the truth, but to make people laugh. I treated my readers as unfairly as I treated everybody else—eager to betray them at the end with some monstrous absurdity or some extravagant anticlimax.

One night, after a lecture in the early days, Tom Fitch, the 'silver-tongued orator of Nevada,' said to me: 'Clemens, your lecture was magnificent. It was eloquent, moving, sincere. Never in my entire life have I listened to such a magnificent piece of descriptive narration. But you committed one unpardonable sin—the unpardonable sin. It is a sin you must never commit again. You closed a most eloquent description, by which you had keyed your audience up to a pitch of the intensest interest, with a piece of atrocious anti-climax which nullified all the really fine effect you had produced. My dear Clemens, whatever you do, never sell your audience.' And that," continued Mr. Clemens, "was my first really profitable lesson."

++++++++++

Mark Twain Speeches: Public Education Association

It is curious to reflect how history repeats itself the world over. Why, I remember the same thing was done when I was a boy on the Mississippi River. There was a proposition in a township there to discontinue public schools because they were too expensive. An old farmer spoke up and said if they stopped the schools they would not save anything, because every time a school was closed a jail had to be built.

It's like feeding a dog on his own tail. He'll never get fat. I believe it is better to support schools than jails.

++++++++++

Mark Twain Speeches: Joan of Arc

And he was that kind of a boy. He should have lived, and yet he should not have lived, because he died at that early age—he couldn't have been more than twenty—he had seen all there was to see in the world that was worth the trouble of living in it; he had seen all of this world that is valuable; he had seen all of this world that was illusion, and illusion, is the only valuable thing in it. He had arrived at that point where presently the illusions would cease and he would have entered upon the realities of life, and God help the man that has arrived at that point.

++++++++++

Mark Twain Speeches: Dinner to Mr. Jerome

You see that. As it stands now, I cannot. I am crippled in that way and to that extent, for I would ever so much like to do it. I am not a Congress, and I cannot distribute pensions, and I don't know any other legitimate way to buy a vote. But if I should think of any legitimate way, I shall make use of it, and then I shall vote for Mr. Jerome.

++++++++++

Mark Twain Speeches: Education and Citizenship

Have you ever thought about this? Is there a college in the whole country where there is a chair of good citizenship? There is a kind of bad citizenship which is taught in the schools, but no real good citizenship taught. There are some which teach insane citizenship, bastard citizenship, but that is all. Patriotism! Yes; but patriotism is usually the refuge of the scoundrel. He is the man who talks the loudest.

++++++++++

Mark Twain Speeches: Taxes and Morals

"I came here in the responsible capacity of policeman to watch Mr. Choate. This is an occasion of grave and serious importance, and it seems necessary for me to be present, so that if he tried to work off any statement that required correction, reduction, refutation, or exposure, there would be a tried friend of the public to protect the house. He has not made one statement whose veracity fails to tally exactly with my own standard. I have never seen a person improve so. This makes me thankful and proud of a country that can produce such men—two such men. And all in the same country. We can't be with you always; we are passing away, and then—well, everything will have to stop, I reckon. It is a sad thought. But in spirit I shall still be with you. Choate, too—if he can.

Every born American among the eighty millions, let his creed or destitution of creed be what it may, is indisputably a Christian—to this degree that his moral constitution is Christian.

There are two kinds of Christian morals, one private and the other public. These two are so distinct, so unrelated, that they are no more akin to each other than are archangels and politicians. During three hundred and sixty-three days in the year the American citizen is true to his Christian private morals, and keeps undefiled the nation's character at its best and highest; then in the other two days of the year he leaves his Christian private morals at home and carries his Christian public morals to the tax office and the polls, and does the best he can to damage and undo his whole year's faithful and righteous work. Without a blush he will vote for an unclean boss if that boss is his party's Moses, without compunction he will vote against the best man in the whole land if he is on the other ticket. Every year in a number of cities and States he helps put corrupt men in office, whereas if he would but throw away his Christian public morals, and carry his Christian private morals to the polls, he could promptly purify the public service and make the possession of office a high and honorable distinction.

Once a year he lays aside his Christian private morals and hires a ferry-boat and piles up his bonds in a warehouse in New Jersey for three days, and gets out his Christian public morals and goes to the tax office and holds up his hands and swears he wishes he may never—never if he's got a cent in the world, so help him. The next day the list appears in the papers—a column and a quarter of names, in fine print, and every man in the list a billionaire and member of a couple of churches. I know all those people. I have friendly, social, and criminal relations with the whole lot of them. They never miss a sermon when they are so's to be around, and they never miss swearing-off day, whether they are so's to be around or not."

++++++++++

Mark Twain Speeches: Dress of a Civilized Woman

"And that reminds me of a trifle. Any time you want to, you can glance around the carpet of a Pullman car, and go and pick up a hair-pin; but not to save your life can you get any woman in that car to acknowledge that hair-pin. Now, isn't that strange? But it's true. The woman who has never swerved from cast-iron veracity and fidelity in her whole life will, when confronted with this crucial test, deny her hair-pin. She will deny that hair-pin before a hundred witnesses. I have stupidly got into more trouble and more hot water trying to hunt up the owner of a hair-pin in a Pullman than by any other indiscretion of my life."

++++++++++

Mark Twain Speeches: Layman's Sermon

I have received recently several letters asking my counsel or advice. The principal request is for some incident that may prove helpful to the young. There were a lot of incidents in my career to help me along—sometimes they helped me along faster than I wanted to go.

Here is such a request. It is a telegram from Joplin, Missouri, and it reads: "In what one of your works can we find the definition of a gentleman?"

I have not answered that telegram, either; I couldn't. It seems to me that if any man has just merciful and kindly instincts he would be a gentleman, for he would need nothing else in the world.

I received the other day a letter from my old friend, William Dean Howells—Howells, the head of American literature. No one is able to stand with him.

He is an old, old friend of mine, and he writes me, "To-morrow I shall be sixty-nine years old." Why, I am surprised at Howells writing that! I have known him longer than that. I'm sorry to see a man trying to appear so young. Let's see. Howells says now, "I see you have been burying Patrick. I suppose he was old, too."

No, he was never old—Patrick. He came to us thirty-six years ago. He was my coachman on the morning that I drove my young bride to our new home.

He was a young Irishman, slender, tall, lithe, honest, truthful, and he never changed in all his life. He really was with us but twenty-five years, for he did not go with us to Europe, but he never regarded that as separation. As the children grew up he was their guide. He was all honor, honesty, and affection. He was with us in New Hampshire, with us last summer, and his hair was just as black, his eyes were just as blue, his form just as straight, and his heart just as good as on the day we first met. In all the long years Patrick never made a mistake. He never needed an order, he never received a command. He knew. I have been asked for my idea of an ideal gentleman, and I give it to you – Patrick McAleer.

++++++++++

Mark Twain: A Biography - Albert Bigelow Paine

The Watterson introduction (at the Lincoln Birthday Celebration, February 11th 1901) is one of the choicest of Mark Twain's speeches—a pure and perfect example of simple eloquence, worthy of the occasion which gave it utterance, worthy in spite of its playful paragraphs (or even because of them, for Lincoln would have loved them), to become the matrix of that imperishable Gettysburg phrase with which he makes his climax. He opened by dwelling for a moment on Colonel Watterson as a soldier, journalist, orator, statesman, and patriot; then he said:

"It is a curious circumstance that without collusion of any kind, but merely in obedience to a strange and pleasant and dramatic freak of destiny, he and I, kinsmen by blood for we are that--and one-time rebels--for we were that--should be chosen out of a million surviving quondam rebels to come here and bare our heads in reverence and love of that noble soul whom 40 years ago we tried with all our hearts and all our strength to defeat and dispossess--Abraham Lincoln!

Is the Rebellion ended and forgotten? Are the Blue and the Gray one to-day? By authority of this sign we may answer yes; there was a Rebellion--that incident is closed.

I was born and reared in a slave State, my father was a slave owner; and in the Civil War I was a second lieutenant in the Confederate service. For a while. This second cousin of mine, Colonel Watterson, the orator of this present occasion, was born and reared in a slave State, was a colonel in the Confederate service, and rendered me such assistance as he could in my self-appointed great task of annihilating the Federal armies and breaking up the Union.

I laid my plans with wisdom and foresight, and if Colonel Watterson had obeyed my orders I should have succeeded in my giant undertaking. It was my intention to drive General Grant into the Pacific--if I could get transportation--and I told Colonel Watterson to surround the Eastern armies and wait till I came. But he was insubordinate, and stood upon a punctilio of military etiquette; he refused to take orders from a second lieutenant--and the Union was saved. This is the first time that this secret has been revealed. Until now no one outside the family has known the facts. But there they stand: Watterson saved the Union. Yet to this day that man gets no pension.

Those were great days, splendid days. What an uprising it was! For the hearts of the whole nation, North and South, were in the war. We of the South were not ashamed, for like the men of the North, we were fighting for what we believed with all our sincere souls to be our rights; on both sides we were fighting for our homes and hearthstones, and for the honor of the flags we loved; and when men fight for these things, and under these convictions, with nothing sordid to tarnish their cause, that cause is holy, the blood spilt for it is sacred, the life that is laid down for it is consecrated.

To-day we no longer regret the result; to-day we are glad it came out as it did; but we are not ashamed that we did our endeavor; we did our bravest best, against despairing odds, for the cause which was precious to us and which our consciences approved: and we are proud--and you are proud-—the kindred blood in your veins answers when I say it--you are proud of the record we made in those mighty collisions in the field.

What an uprising it was! We did not have to supplicate for soldiers on either side. "We are coming, Father Abraham, three hundred thousand strong!" That was the music North and South. The very choicest young blood and brawn and brain rose up from Maine to the Gulf and flocked to the standards-- just as men always do when in their eyes their cause is great and fine and their hearts are in it; just as men flocked to the Crusades, sacrificing all they possessed to the cause, and entering cheerfully upon hardships which we cannot even imagine in this age, and upon toilsome and wasting journeys which in our time would be the equivalent of circumnavigating the globe five times over.

North and South we put our hearts into that colossal struggle, and out of it came the blessed fulfilment of the prophecy of the immortal Gettysburg speech which said: "We here highly resolve that these dead shall not have died in vain; that this nation, under God, shall have a new birth of freedom; and that a government of the people, by the people, for the people, shall not perish from the earth."

We are here to honor the birthday of the greatest citizen, and the noblest and the best, after Washington, that this land or any other has yet produced. The old wounds are healed, you and we are brothers again; you testify it by honoring two of us- -once soldiers of the Lost Cause, and foes of your great and good leader--with the privilege of assisting here; and we testify it by laying our honest homage at the feet of Abraham Lincoln, and in forgetting that you of the North and we of the South were ever enemies, and remembering only that we are now indistinguishably fused together and nameable by one common great name--Americans!

++++++++++

Mark Twain Speeches: Woman – A Eulogy of the Fair Sex.

(According to biographer Paine, this is the first of Mark Twain's after-dinner speeches to be preserved. Here is how it was reported the following day – January 13, 1868)

The Washington Correspondents Club held its anniversary on Saturday night. Mr. Clemens, better known as Mark Twain, responded to the toast, "Woman, the pride of the professions and the jewel of ours." He said:

Mr. President,—I do not know why I should have been singled out to receive the greatest distinction of the evening—for so the office of replying to the toast to woman has been regarded in every age. [Applause.] I do not know why I have received this distinction, unless it be that I am a trifle less homely than the other members of the club. But, be this as it may, Mr. President, I am proud of the position, and you could not have chosen any one who would have accepted it more gladly, or labored with a heartier goodwill to do the subject justice, than I. Because, Sir, I love the sex. [Laughter.] I love all the women, sir, irrespective of age or color. [Laughter.]

Human intelligence cannot estimate what we owe to woman, sir. She sews on our buttons [laughter]; she mends our clothes [laughter]; she ropes us in at the church fairs; she confides in us; she tells us whatever she can find out about the private affairs of the neighbors; she gives good advice, and plenty of it; she gives us a piece of her mind sometimes—and sometimes all of it; she soothes our aching brows; she bears our children...... Ours as a general thing.

In all relations of life, sir, it is but just and a graceful tribute to woman to say of her that she is a brick. [Great laughter.]

Wheresoever you place woman, sir—in whatsoever position or estate—she is an ornament to that place she occupies, and a treasure to the world. [Here Mr. Twain paused, looked inquiringly at his hearers, and remarked that the applause should come in at this point. It came in. Mr. Twain resumed his eulogy.] Look at the noble names of history! Look at Cleopatra! Look at Desdemona! Look at Florence Nightingale! Look at Joan of Arc! Look at Lucretia Borgia! [Disapprobation expressed. "Well," said Mr. Twain, scratching his head, doubtfully, "suppose we let Lucretia slide."] Look at Joyce Heth! Look at Mother Eve! I repeat, sir, look at the illustrious names of

61

history! Look at the Widow Machree! Look at Lucy Stone! Look at Elizabeth Cady Stanton! Look at George Francis Train! [Great laughter.] And, sir, I say with bowed head and deepest veneration, look at the mother of Washington! She raised a boy that could not lie—could not lie. [Applause.] But he never had any chance. It might have been different with him if he had belonged to a newspaper correspondents' club. [Laughter, groans, hisses, cries of "put him out." Mark looked around placidly upon his excited audience, and resumed.]

I repeat, sir, that in whatsoever position you place a woman she is an ornament to society and a treasure to the world. As a sweetheart she has few equals and no superior [laughter]; as a cousin she is convenient; as a wealthy grandmother with an incurable distemper she is precious; as a wet nurse she has no equal among men! [Laughter.]

What, sir, would the people of this earth be without woman? They would be scarce, sir. Mighty scarce. Then let us cherish her, let us protect her, let us give her our support, our encouragement, our sympathy—ourselves, if we get a chance. [Laughter.]

But, jesting aside, Mr. President, woman is lovable, gracious, kind of heart, beautiful; worthy of all respect, of all esteem, of all deference. Not any here will refuse to drink her health right cordially, for each and every one of us has personally known, loved, and honored the very best one of them all—his own mother! [Applause.]

++++++++++ ++++++++++ ++++++++++

LESSONS: Know your Objective

LESSON I: Begin with the End in Mind

Although recognized internationally as a great humorist, Mark Twain early in his career, realized his role was to provide more than mere humor.

In Toronto, Canada, Twain was full of angst despite a presentation that had brought the house down. He told his good friend and fellow speaker George Washington Cable, "Oh, Cable, I am demeaning myself. I am allowing myself to be a mere buffoon. It's ghastly. I can't endure it any longer." (Cable and Twain toured in 1884/1885 in what was humbly advertised as the "Twins of Genius" tour.)

At the memorial for the great humorist on November 30th 1910, Cable recalled that Twain then, "rehearsed, and rehearsed, and rehearsed, and the next night he gave them a program which he chose to begin, at my suggestion, with the Blue Jay's Message. He left that house as happy as any one ever saw Mark Twain, and that was with a feeling of acute joy because he had won friends he considered worthy."

As with Twain, you need to have a clear idea what the objective is for your speech. A simple but effective exercise that a wise old man "learned" me is to write the objective of your speech on the back of your business card – in ONE sentence. That one sentence is your guiding light. As you develop your speech, refer to that one sentence continuously and ask "Is what I am saying reinforcing my objective?" If not, you are either off track or you need to redefine your objective.

LESSON II: Know what you want to Audience to Do, Feel, Think when you are Finished

A very basic question to ask yourself, the event planner or your sponsor as you prepare your material is "What should the audience do, feel, think when I have finished speaking?"

Clarity on that will help you craft appropriate material, words, phrases and imagery to support your objective.

For instance, if invited to speak to a company that is in dire financial trouble, the same scenario might elicit the following options:

You can turn things around

You are all in this together

You are in serious trouble
You are likely to lose your job

Hopefully, you will be minded to go for option I (the most positive spin). In presenting "You can turn things around, you will craft material, anecdotes and examples that are likely to be quite different to option IV which involves job loss. It is quite likely that turning things around may involve job loss, but if you want your audience to believe in a viable future, to feel they have a chance of survival, your message will reflect those sentiments. True, they may still leave feeling somewhat dubious and uncertain, but that is much better than leaving with the belief they will lose their jobs.

++++++++++ ++++++++++ ++++++++++

How I Implement all that Learnin'!

Know Your Objective

When writing my book *SHEIFGAB! Staying Sane, Motivated and Productive in Job Search*, a wise colleague asked me, "Have you written the back cover?"

"Heck, no, I want to write the book first, then I'll get around to writing the back then."

"You've got it the wrong way round, Conor," she said. "The back cover states what the book is about. Write that first and it will provide you with a clear focus and framework for the book."

"Huh," I thought, "I knew she was a wise colleague!"

That exercise actually changed the title of my book. An earlier title read *SHEIFGAB! Eight Building Blocks to Successful Job Transition* (SHEIFGAB is an acronym for the eight building blocks). That title is clear, but what I really wanted to do in the book was provide solid, implementable ideas to help job seekers stay sane, motivated and productive during a very tough time. That thought process led to a much clearer objective for me and helped me complete a book of which I am very proud. Writing the back cover was akin to writing my objective and I thought it a little ironic that I had not been following the advice I give to speechmakers – Begin with the end in mind.

It isn't good enough to say "I want to make a speech." That is only half the sentence. What you need to say is "I want to make a speech about..." or "I want to make a speech which will..." Likewise, it isn't good enough to say "I want to be a professional speaker." You need to expand that to "I want to be a professional speaker who offers the following benefit and result..."

When writing your speech, the simplest to get you on the correct path is to write that one liner on the back of a business card and refer to it constantly. As with my book cover example, it may take time to actually figure out your ultimate objective. Quite honestly, your objective may even change as you develop your thought process, but if it does, rewrite your objective, so that when someone asks "What is the speech about?, you have a clear, consistent response.

The last thing you want is to fall into the trap of "Having lost sight of our objectives, we redoubled our efforts!"

As a professional speaker, my process involves asking the client in a number of different ways:

What is the purpose of the event?

Why have you hired me?

What balance of Substance / Humor do you want?

What do you want the audience to do, feel, think, after I have completed my keynote?

Then in finalizing conversation with the client, I repeat what she has said, particularly about what "you want the audience to do, feel, think, after I have completed my keynote."

Those answers are the opening lines in my client file, answers I constantly refer to as I go through my speech development. It is my equivalent of the back of business card exercise.

While rehearsing my material, I ask questions like:

"Will this anecdote, reference, quote reinforce my core message, or is it only being dropped in to show how clever I am?" "What experiences can I convey that will relate to my audience and improve the connection and learning?"

It is quite normal to have ongoing email communication with the client in the weeks and months leading up to the engagement, but it is a practice of mine to verbally connect with the client about ten days before the event to chat through the event, get a final briefing on what is happening on the client side e.g. has anything changed in terms of morale, results, successes, hiring, firing etc. and I also reiterate what the cient wants "the audience to do, feel, think, after I have completed my keynote."

++++++++++ ++++++++++ ++++++++++

CHAPTER V

T - Titter, Humor and Laughter

Against the assault of laughter, nothing can stand.

Mark Twain

67

V

*What Mark Twain Learned me 'bout **Titter, Humor and Laughter***

♦ Self-deprecating humor is powerful

♦ You can make (gentle) fun of your audience

♦ Politicians and celebrities are fertile source for humor

♦ Surprise is the bedrock of humor

♦ Exaggeration and Repetition are powerful humor tools

++++++++++ ++++++++++ ++++++++++

Eruption

Humor must not professedly teach, and it must not professedly preach, but it must do both if it would live forever.

++++++++++

How to Tell a Story

The humorous story is told gravely; the teller does his best to conceal the fact that he even dimly suspects that there is anything funny about it.

++++++++++

What Paul Bourget Thinks of Us

Humor is the great thing, the saving thing after all. The minute it crops up, all our hardnesses yield, all our irritations, and resentments flit away, and a sunny spirit takes their place.

++++++++++

*Editorial on appointment as Editor of the Buffalo Express –
August 1869*

Being a stranger, it would be immodest for me to suddenly
and violently assume the associate editorship of the *Buffalo
Express* without a single word of comfort or encouragement to
the unoffending patrons of the paper, who are about to be ex-
posed to constant attacks of my wisdom and learning. But the
word shall be as brief as possible. I only want to assure parties
having a friendly interest in the prosperity of the journal that
I am not going to hurt the paper deliberately and intentionally
at any time. I am not going to introduce any startling reforms,
nor in any way attempt to make trouble....

I shall not make use of slang and vulgarity upon any occasion or under any circumstances, and shall never use pro-
fanity except when discussing house rent and taxes. Indeed,
upon a second thought, I shall not use it even then, for it is
unchristian, inelegant, and degrading; though, to speak truly,
I do not see how house rent and taxes are going to be discussed
worth a cent without it.

I shall not often meddle with politics, because we have a
political Editor who is already excellent and only needs to serve
a term or two in the penitentiary to be perfect. I shall not write
any poetry unless I conceive a spite against the subscribers.
Such is my platform. I do not see any use in it, but custom is
law and must be obeyed.

++++++++++

Mark Twain Speeches: Billiards

The game of billiards has destroyed my naturally sweet
disposition. Once, when I was an underpaid reporter in Vir-
ginia City, whenever I wished to play billiards I went out to
look for an easy mark. One day a stranger came to town and
opened a billiard parlor. I looked him over casually. When he
proposed a game, I answered, "All right."

"Just knock the balls around a little so that I can get your
gait," he said; and when I had done so, he remarked: "I will be
perfectly fair with you. I'll play you left-handed." I felt hurt, for

he was cross-eyed, freckled, and had red hair, and I determined to teach him a lesson. He won first shot, ran out, took my half-dollar, and all I got was the opportunity to chalk my cue.

"If you can play like that with your left hand," I said, "I'd like to see you play with your right."

"I can't," he said. "I'm left-handed."

++++++++++

Mark Twain Speeches: Seventieth Birthday

I have made it a rule never to smoke more than one cigar at a time. I have no other restriction as regards smoking. .... As an example to others, and—not that I care for moderation myself, it has always been my rule never to smoke when asleep, and never to refrain when awake. It is a good rule. I mean, for me; but some of you know quite well that it wouldn't answer for everybody that's trying to get to be seventy.

I smoke in bed until I have to go to sleep; I wake up in the night, sometimes once, sometimes twice; sometimes three times, and I never waste any of these opportunities to smoke. This habit is so old and dear and precious to me that I would feel as you, sir, would feel if you should lose the only moral you've got—meaning the chairman—if you've got one: I am making no charges: I will grant, here, that I have stopped smoking now and then, for a few months at a time, but it was not on principle, it was only to show off; it was to pulverize those critics who said I was a slave to my habits and couldn't break my bonds.

++++++++++

Mark Twain: Archibald Henderson

In Boston, when asked what he thought about the existence of a heaven or a hell, he looked grave for a moment, and then replied: "I don't want to express an opinion. It's policy for me to keep silent. You see, I have friends in both places.

71

++++++++++

Following the Equator: Pudd'nhead Wilson's New Calendar

SATAN (impatiently) to NEWCOMER. The trouble with you Chicago people is, that you think you are the best people down here; whereas you are merely the most numerous.

++++++++++

Mark Twain Speeches: Business

My idea is that the employer should be the busy man, and the employee the idle one. The employer should be the worried man, and the employee the happy one. And why not? He gets the salary. My plan is to get another man to do the work for me. In that there's more repose. What I want is repose first, last, and all the time............

My axiom is, to succeed in business: avoid my example.

++++++++++

Mark Twain Speeches: Unconscious Plagiarism

That is what a teaspoonful of brains will do for a man—and admirers had often told me I had nearly a basketful—though they were rather reserved as to the size of the basket.

++++++++++

Mark Twain Speeches: To the Whitefriars (London)

And here, we three (friends) meet again as exiles on one pretext or another, and you will notice that while we are absent there is a pleasing tranquility in America—a building up of public confidence. We are doing the best we can for our country. I think we have spent our lives in serving our country, and we never serve it to greater advantage than when we get out of it.

++++++++++

Mark Twain Speeches: The Savage Club Dinner

Stanley apparently carried a book of mine feloniously away to Africa, and I have not a doubt that it had a noble and up-lifting influence there in the wilds of Africa—because on his previous journeys he never carried anything to read except Shakespeare and the Bible. I did not know of that circumstance. I did not know that he had carried a book of mine. I only noticed that when he came back he was a reformed man............

I am not one of those who in expressing opinions confine themselves to facts. I don't know anything that mars good literature so completely as too much truth. Facts contain a deal of poetry, but you can't use too many of them without damaging your literature.

++++++++++

Mark Twain Speeches: Disappearance of Literature

Professor Winchester also said something about there being no modern epics like *Paradise Lost*. I guess he's right. He talked as if he was pretty familiar with that piece of literary work, and nobody would suppose that he never had read it. I don't believe any of you have ever read *Paradise Lost*, and you don't want to. That's something that you just want to take on trust. It's a classic, just as Professor Winchester says, and it meets his definition of a classic—something that everybody wants to have read and nobody wants to read.

++++++++++

Mark Twain Speeches: The Old Fashioned Printer

He had changed his mind, which was a gilded figure of speech, because he hadn't any.

++++++++++

73

Mark Twain Speeches: Accident Insurance

Certainly there is no nobler field for human effort than the insurance line of business—especially accident insurance. Ever since I have been a director in an accident-insurance company I have felt that I am a better man. Life has seemed more precious. Accidents have assumed a kindlier aspect. Distressing special providences have lost half their horror. I look upon a cripple now with affectionate interest—as an advertisement. I do not seem to care for poetry any more. I do not care for politics—even agriculture does not excite me. But to me now there is a charm about a railway collision that is unspeakable.

++++++++++

Mark Twain Speeches: Sixty-Seventh Birthday

No modest person, and I was born one, can talk on compliments. A man gets up and is filled to the eyes with happy emotions, but his tongue is tied; he has nothing to say; he is in the condition of Doctor Rice's friend who came home drunk and explained it to his wife, and his wife said to him, "John, when you have drunk all the whiskey you want, you ought to ask for sarsaparilla." He said, "Yes, but when I have drunk all the whiskey I want, I can't say sarsaparilla." And so I think it is much better to leave a man unmolested until the testimony and pleadings are all in. Otherwise he is dumb—he is at the sarsaparilla stage.

++++++++++

Mark Twain Speeches: The Savage Club Dinner

It is very seldom in a day that I am seventy-two years old. I am older now sometimes than I was when I used to rob orchards; a thing which I would not do to-day—if the orchards were watched.

++++++++++

Mark Twain Speeches: When in Doubt, Tell the Truth

I was so relieved when judge Leventritt did find something that was not taxable—when he said that the commissioner could not tax your patience. And that comforted me. We've got so much taxation. I don't know of a single foreign product that enters this country untaxed except the answer to prayer.

++++++++++

Letter to W. D. Howells

Jane (Austen) is entirely impossible. It seems a great pity that they allowed her to die a natural death.

++++++++++

Following the Equator

Jane Austen's books, too, are absent from this library. Just that one omission alone would make a fairly good library out of a library that hadn't a book in it.

++++++++++

Mark Twain Speeches: Princeton

It is not my purpose to lecture any more as long as I live. I never intend to stand up on a platform any more—unless by the request of a sheriff or something like that.

++++++++++

Mark Twain Speeches: Morals and Memory

It's my opinion that everyone I know has morals, though I wouldn't like to ask. I know I have. But I'd rather teach them than practice them any day. "Give them to others"—that's my motto. Then you never have any use for them when you're left without.

++++++++++

75

Mark Twain Speeches: Spelling and Pictures

So I never write 'metropolis' for seven cents, because I can get the same money for 'city.' I never write 'policeman,' because I can get the same price for 'cop.' And so on and so on. I never write 'valetudinarian' at all, for not even hunger and wretchedness can humble me to the point where I will do a word like that for seven cents; I wouldn't do it for fifteen. Examine your obscene text, please; count the words.

++++++++++

Mark Twain Speeches: Society of American Authors

He started in, in the way that I knew I should be painted with all sincerity, and was leading to things that would not be to my credit; but when he said that he never read a book of mine I knew at once that he was a liar, because he never could have had all the wit and intelligence with which he was blessed unless he had read my works as a basis.

++++++++++

Mark Twain Speeches: Literature

I propose to go there to purify the political atmosphere. I am in favor of everything everybody is in favor of. What you should do is to satisfy the whole nation, not half of it, for then you would only be half a President.

There could not be a broader platform than mine. I am in favor of anything and everything—of temperance and intemperance, morality and qualified immorality, gold standard and free silver.

++++++++++

Mark Twain Speeches: Tammany and Croker

The election makes me think of a story of a man who was dying. He had only two minutes to live, so he sent for a clergyman and asked him, "Where is the best place to go to?" He was undecided about it. So the minister told him that each place had its advantages—heaven for climate, and hell for society.

++++++++++

Mark Twain Speeches: Address to Young Girls

I don't know what to tell you girls to do. Mr. Martin has told you everything you ought to do, and now I must give you some don'ts.

There are three things which come to my mind which I consider excellent advice:

First, girls, don't smoke—that is, don't smoke to excess. I am seventy-three and a half years old, and have been smoking seventy-three of them. But I never smoke to excess—that is, I smoke in moderation, only one cigar at a time.

Second, don't drink—that is, don't drink to excess.

Third, don't marry—I mean, to excess.

Honesty is the best policy. That is an old proverb; but you don't want ever to forget it in your journey through life.

++++++++++

Mark Twain Speeches: Our Children and Great Discoveries

And there was once another great discoverer—I've forgotten his name, and I don't remember what he discovered, but I know it was something very important, and I hope you will all tell your children about it when you get home.

++++++++++

Mark Twain Speeches: The Babies

As long as you are in your right mind don't you ever pray for twins. Twins amount to a permanent riot. And there ain't any real difference between triplets and an insurrection.

++++++++++

Mark Twain Speeches: The Weather

You fix up for the drought; you leave your umbrella in the house and sally out, and two to one you get drowned. You make up your mind that the earthquake is due; you stand from under, and take hold of something to steady yourself, and the first thing you know you get struck by. These are great disappointments; but they can't be helped. The lightning there is peculiar; it is so convincing, that when it strikes a thing it doesn't leave enough of that thing behind for you to tell whether—Well, you'd think it was something valuable, and a Congressman had been there.

++++++++++

Mark Twain Speeches: Robert Fulton Fund

"There was a mystery," said I. "We were twins, and one day when we were two weeks old—that is, he was one week old, and I was one week old—we got mixed up in the bath-tub, and one of us drowned. We never could tell which. One of us had a strawberry birthmark on the back of his hand. There it is on my hand. This is the one that was drowned. There's no doubt about it.

++++++++++

Mark Twain – A Biography: Albert Bigelow Paine

I had great presence of mind once. It was at a fire. An old man leaned out of a four-story building, calling for help. Everybody in the crowd below looked up, but nobody did anything. The ladders weren't long enough. Nobody had any presence of mind–nobody but me. I came to the rescue. I yelled for a rope. When it came I threw the old man the end of it. He caught it, and I told him to tie it around his waist. He did so, and I pulled him down.

++++++++++

Mark Twain on Politics and Politicians

Twain had little respect for politicians and wrote scathingly of them. He often poked fun at good friends who had entered the political arena, but he reserved a particularly acerbic wit for those in Congress.

++++++++++

Mark Twain Speeches: Welcome Home

The greatest Missourian of them all—here he sits—Tom Reed, who has always concealed his birth till now. And since I have been away I know what has been happening in his case: he has deserted politics, and now is leading a creditable life. He has reformed, and God prosper him.

++++++++++

Mark Twain Speeches: Welcome Home

And then we have taken Chauncey Depew out of a useful and active life and made him a Senator—embalmed him, corked him up. And I am not grieving. That man has said many a true thing about me in his time, and I always said something would happen to him. Look at that [pointing to Mr. Depew] gilded mummy! He has made my life a sorrow to me at many a banquet on both sides of the ocean, and now he has got it. Perish the hand that pulls that cork!

++++++++++

What Is Man?

Fleas can be taught nearly anything that a Congressman can.

++++++++++

Mark Twain Speeches: To the Whitefriars

"When I look upon the inspiring face of Mr. Depew, it carries me a long way back. An old and valued friend of mine is

79

he, and I saw his career as it came along, and it has reached pretty well up to now, when he, by another miscarriage of justice, is a United States Senator. But those were delightful days when I was taking lessons in oratory."

++++++++++

Mark Twain Notebook

Whiskey is taken into the committee rooms in demijohns and carried out in demagogues.

++++++++++

Mark Twain Speeches: Municipal Corruption

Principles aren't of much account anyway, except at election time. After that you hang them up to let them season.

++++++++++

Letter fragment, 1891

Congress: The smallest minds and the selfishest souls and the cowardliest hearts that God makes.

++++++++++

Mark Twain - A Biography: Albert Bigelow Paine

Suppose you were an idiot. And suppose you were a member of Congress. But I repeat myself.

++++++++++

Autobiography of Mark Twain

All Congresses and Parliaments have a kindly feeling for idiots, and a compassion for them, on account of personal experience and heredity.

++++++++++

Eruption

Few men of first class ability can afford to let their affairs go to ruin while they fool away their time in Legislatures...But your chattering, one-horse village lawyer likes it, and your solemn ass from the cow countries, who don't know the Constitution from the Lord's Prayer, enjoys it, and these you always find in the Assembly; the one gabble, gabble, gabbling threadbare platitudes and 'give-me-liberty-or give-me-death' buncombe from morning to night, and the other asleep, with his slab-soled brogans set up like a couple of grave-stones on the top of his desk.

++++++++++

Following the Equator: Pudd'nhead Wilson's New Calendar

It could probably be shown by facts and figures that there is no distinctly native American criminal class except Congress.

++++++++++

Eruption

There are many Senators whom I hold in a certain respect and would not think of declining to meet socially, if I believed it was the will of God. We have lately sent a United States Senator to the penitentiary, but I am quite well aware that of those who have escaped this promotion there are several who are in some regards guiltless of crime--not guiltless of all crimes, for that cannot be said of any United States Senator, I think, but guiltless of some kinds of crime

++++++++++

New York Tribune, 10 March 1873

I never can think of Judas Iscariot without losing my temper. To my mind Judas Iscariot was nothing but a low, mean, premature, Congressman.

++++++++++

Letter to J. H. Twichell, 2/16/1905

We are insane, each in our own way, and with insanity goes irresponsibility. Theodore (Roosevelt) the man is sane; in fairness we ought to keep in mind that Theodore, as statesman and politician, is insane and irresponsible.

++++++++++

Eruption

"Mr. Roosevelt is the Tom Sawyer of the political world of the twentieth century; always showing off; always hunting for a chance to show off; in his frenzied imagination the Great Republic is a vast Barnum circus with him for a clown and the whole world for audience; he would go to Halifax for half a chance to show off and he would go to hell for a whole one."

++++++++++

Mark Twain – A Biography: Albert Bigelow Paine

If those burglars that broke into my house....had broken into this library they would have read a few books and led a better life. Now they are in jail, and if they keep on they will go to Congress. When a person starts downhill you can never tell where he's going to stop.

++++++++++ ++++++++++ ++++++++++

LESSONS: Titter, Humor and Laughter

LESSON I: Self-deprecating Humor Wins the Audience

If you want to be liked, make fun of yourself, not the audience. Mark Twain was often self-deprecating as in his "basketful of brains" comment. In *Innocents Abroad* he wrote "I must have a prodigious quantity of mind; it takes me as much as a week sometimes to make it up."

There is no guaranteed formula for making an audience laugh, but the speaker who is not afraid to laugh at himself is much more likely to get his audience laughing with him.

Tell your audience when you were a knucklehead or did something that would not qualify you for Mensa! Not only will you have them laughing, but they will also relate better to you because you are coming across as "ordinary" and down to earth.

Tell them you are wonderful and the audience will wait for you to fall from your pedestal. Tell them (through your tone, manner and demeanor) that you are one of them, ordinary and down to earth and they may will put you on a pedestal.

LESSON II: You Can Make Gentle Fun of your Audience

Once you have made fun of yourself, it is then acceptable to make fun of your audience. In fairness, this assumes that you have researched your Audience, Know your Objective, the mood and morale of those in front of you.

For instance having worked the room, you can determine if there is someone in the audience you can gently rib. The level of ribbing depends on who you are speaking to. The type of humor also varies. Without being blue or offensive, you can probably make comments to a construction sales force that you will not be able to make to the Catholic Mothers of Seven. Remember the Golden Rule of humor: If in doubt, leave it out!

When working with a group of people you know well, there is little danger that you will offend or upset someone but when presenting to a new audience, be very careful.

Sport is an easy way to have fun with your audience – e.g. "I know we are here in New York, home of the Yankees (big cheer from audience), but come on, wouldn't you much prefer to live in Chicago, home of the unbelievable Cubs?" At this stage, you should be getting good humored boos from the audience and probably shouts of "Losers."

Play with your audience when appropriate. Have fun with them and they will have fun with you.

LESSON III: Politicians and Celebrities are Fertile Source for Humor

Although a lovely man to his public, Mark Twain was not one you wished to offend. He had an acerbic wit often aimed at politicians. Late night comedy shows follow the Twain formula, understanding that if someone is in the public eye long enough, they will provide fertile source for humor. Did someone mention Sarah Palin, George Bush, Joe Biden, Kanye West, the Kardashians?

Given little time and effort, it is relatively easy to make fun of anyone in Washington. I mean, let's face it, if we didn't laugh at them, we would simply break down and cry!

But you don't have to always develop your own material. Use quotes and anecdotes from the greatest humorist of all, Mark Twain. Obviously, some of his excellent material is in this book, but if you don't like what you see here, Google "Twain quotes" for a raft of material that should be relevant and humorous for any event or occasion.

More specifically Google "jokes about..." or "quotes about." When you find something appropriate, do give credit—"As Groucho Marx said "Marriage is the chief cause of divorce."" (Totally out of context, but you get the point, I hope.)

When you hear a political or celebrity joke from late night hosts Jimmy Kimmel or Seth Meyers that gets you laughing, stop and ask yourself, "Why was that funny?" Over time, you will realize most of the jokes about today's politicians are basic rehashes of jokes told about George Bush, Bill Clinton, and Richard Nixon etc.

If you wish to have a better understanding of comedy writing, add a few more dollars to Judy Carter's bank account and buy the excellent *The Comedy Bible*.

Remember the words of a very wise man:

"Against the assault of laughter, nothing can stand."

++++++++++ ++++++++++ ++++++++++

How I Implement all that Learnin'!

Titter, Humor and Laughter

The speaker droned on and on and on, until finally an audience member tossed a program at him, but missed, hitting one of the fellow panelists on the stage, dozing in boredom, who cried out, "What did you do that for? I was doing fine."

We have all been there, wondering when or if the speaker would ever end, even praying that the house lights will fail.

Almost (not) all speeches benefit from the addition of humor and fun. As a speaker, my Brand Promise is E4: Energize, Educate, Entertain and Easy to work with. I do this by providing Substance with Humor. I never position myself as a comedian and quickly correct anyone who says I am. In one sense it is a nice compliment, but a comedian is a much more difficult job than a humorist and quite honestly, on the speaking circuit, is generally not as lucrative.

You're a Natural!

I am blessed to see the humor in a lot of things, but smile when, for instance, after completing an Emcee presentation, someone says, "You're a natural and really quick-witted."

Oh, Yeah! Believe it or not, that comment bugs me, because I probably spent hours that week, researching, writing and rehearsing customized material to be "a natural."

It would not be an exaggeration to say that the majority of the witticisms I throw out "spontaneously" are crafted prior to the event. My process is to review the agenda, read the profile of each speaker, research their topic and message in some detail, then prepare some "impromptu" remarks.

One of the larger files in my email system is titled "Fun Stuff." Whenever someone sends me a joke, humorous story, cartoon etc. that email goes to "Fun stuff." I admit that the emails I get from my brothers are probably not suitable for a conference, unless I'm speaking to a group of Longshoremen from New Jersey and even then......!

Note, I am not encouraging you to steal anyone's material, but much of what you receive can be adapted and customized to your particular situation, particularly quotes and anecdotes related to politicians and celebrities.

Let's assume I'm doing the previously mentioned Widget conference. Google searches I might do include:

Jokes about widgets

Widget cartoons

Humorous headlines widgets

Groucho Marx / Mark Twain / Will Rogers / Widgets

Famous widget people

Widget Jargon

I prefer to tell humorous anecdotes rather than jokes, but I sometimes will adapt a joke to provide a lesson or moral.

Should you start your speech with a joke? My answer is a definitive No / Yes / Maybe! That clarifies things a lot, doesn't it? I'll try and be clearer. It depends! There are no definites, but if you tell a joke, make sure it is funny for that audience. If it bombs, you will immediately feel under pressure.

I generally tell my humorous stories (some quite lengthy) to make a serious point. Anecdotes are based on personal experiences e.g. when one of Illinois' finest wished to (ahem) engage me in conversation over my failure to stop at a "slightly red light!" I can spin that yarn out for six minutes, but there is a moral to it which is that when things go wrong, ask yourself the question, "What do I want my Attitude to be?"

This story about the "Mobile Disco" (cop car, flashing lights) is a "signature story" of mine. I don't have a recording of the original version, but it was considerably shorter than six minutes. Over time, the story developed legs, e.g. I might make a genuinely spontaneous quip which gets laughter, so what happens the next time? The line goes in.

When speaking to Healthcare, Oncology, Nursing groups I recall when "I went into hospital for prostate surgery with a new pair of Monty Python pajamas (here I pause because I know the audience will laugh), yes, pajamas bearing the legend "It's just a flesh wound!"" (More laughter.)

You will eventually get to know and anticipate what the audience will laugh at, which audiences laugh more (Nurses are a blast to work with) and the timing for each humorous comment to take effect.

Political Humor

Mark Twain loved to make fun of politicians, mainly because he considered the majority of them to be "idiots." I doubt whether anything happening today would change his mind.

Given my interest in political biography, my library has a lot of political material. These books are covered in Post-It notes highlighting references, anecdotes, goofs, anything that takes my fancy. I don't know when or if I will use the material, but it is there.

Interesting material I read online goes into a file titled "Interesting thoughts for a damp day!" Don't ask! Today, I have a treasure trove of anecdotes, quotes, goofs by politicians and celebrities. With very little effort, I can introduce humorous anecdotes about Presidents Reagan, Carter, Bush I & II, Kennedy, Lyndon Johnson, Teddy Roosevelt, FDR, Warren Harding and believe it or not - Richard Nixon!

The following are some specifics that will help you add humor to your speech.

1) **L**isten. You may not realize it, but you probably said something today that got a laugh. In future, deliberately listen for that laughter, take note of it. Developing this habit will ultimately provide you with good material.

2) **A**necdotes. Capture stories, anecdotes that make you smile. You never know when you will find them useful.

3) **U**ncomfortable. Recall incidents that were once uncomfortable for you, but which you now regale friends about over coffee or lunch. Exaggerate that story a little with carefully chosen words and you have humor gold.

4) **G**oogle. ('nuff said!)

5) **H**ee, Hee, Hee. The next time you hear a "Hee, Hee, Hee," you have the seed for a "Ho, Ho, Ho." Now, water that seed of laughter. Write, rewrite, improve the punch line and the story telling so that next time, you will have 'em laughing hysterically.

Five simple useful practices that coincidentally generate the acronym "LAUGH." Funny!

++++++++++ ++++++++++ ++++++++++

CHAPTER VI

W - Wait (The Pause)

The right word may be effective but no word was ever as effective as a rightly timed pause.

Mark Twain

VI

*What Mark Twain Learned me 'bout **Wait and the Pause***

- ♦ No word is as effective as the rightly timed pause
- ♦ Silence does speak volumes
- ♦ Every speech can benefit from selective pausing
- ♦ The effective pause requires confidence and practice

++++++++++ ++++++++++ ++++++++++

Mark Twain: How to Tell a Story

The pause is an exceedingly important feature in any kind of story, and a frequently recurring feature, too. It is a dainty thing, and delicate, and also uncertain and treacherous; for it must be exactly the right length - no more and no less - or it fails of its purpose and makes trouble.

If the pause is too short the impressive point is passed, and [and if too long] the audience have had time to divine that a surprise is intended—and then you can't surprise them, of course.

On the platform I used to tell a ghost story that had a pause in front of the snapper on the end, and that pause was the most important thing in the whole story.

If I got it the right length precisely, I could spring the finishing ejaculation with effect enough to make some impressible girl deliver a startled little yelp and jump out of her seat—and that was what I was after.

++++++++++

The Syracuse Daily Standard, December 7 1871

MARK TWAIN.-- An immense audience assembled at Wieting Opera House last evening to make the acquaintance of this celebrated humorist. Mr. Clemens's subject was Artemus Ward. His tribute to the genius and untimely end of the genial proprietor of the "great moral wax figgers" had at times a touch of genuine pathos while at the same time it was replete with humorous anecdotes concerning the lamented Artemus (Ward) and quotations from his writings. Mark resembles the subject of his lecture in one respect -- his pauses are more eloquent than his words. As it is impossible to report a pause, while to leave out these "brilliant flashes of silence" would be to spoil the lecture, we shall not attempt to reproduce it.

++++++++++

Mark Twain – A Biography: Albert Bigelow Paine

His delivery was described as a "long, monotonous drawl, with the fun invariably coming in at the end of a sentence—after a pause."

++++++++++

Autobiography of Mark Twain

That impressive silence, that eloquent silence, that geometrically progressive silence which often achieves a desired effect where no combination of words howsoever felicitous could accomplish it.

++++++++++

Mark Twain Speeches: Books, Authors and Hats

I have suffered since I have been in this town; in the first place, right away, when I came here, from a newsman going around with a great red, highly displayed placard in the place of an apron. He was selling newspapers, and there were two sentences on that placard which would have been all right if they had been punctuated; but they ran those two sentences together without a comma or anything, and that would naturally create a wrong impression, because it said, "Mark Twain arrives Ascot Cup stolen." No doubt many a person was misled by those sentences joined together in that unkind way. I have no doubt my character has suffered from it. I suppose I ought to defend my character, but how can I defend it? I can say here and now—and anybody can see by my face that I am sincere, that I speak the truth—that I have never seen that Cup. I have not got the Cup—I did not have a chance to get it.

++++++++++

The New York Times, March 31, 1907

"You attribute much of your success in telling the story to the pause before the last words, do you not?" asked the reporter

"There is a knack in telling such a story," Mr. Clemens replied. "You must know exactly how long to hold your audience before coming to the point of the joke. After some experience I could tell how long the pause should be to the moment. The length of such a pause differs from time to time and with different audiences. Circumstances may alter it. Even such a little thing as a person coughing in an audience will hurry the point."

"It is the same principle, then that governs an actor when he gains the attention of an audience by moving, or 'holding a scene,' as he calls it?"

"That is the idea exactly. One of the best examples I remember was Mr. Herne's acting in the last scene of 'Shore Acres.' You remember there was a long silence before the curtain fell. The actor's movements and expression were telling the story. Then came the final moment - an absolute pause, a final impression conveyed by it. That is the best way I can illustrate the value of a pause."

++++++++++

Harpers Magazine article by Albert Bigelow Paine on the Tribute speech to Ulysses S. Grant - The Babies. (Twain started his speech at two in the morning and was the FIFTEENTH speaker!)

Clemens's own speech came last. He had been placed at the end to hold the house. He was preceded by a dull speaker, and his heart sank, for it was two o'clock (a.m.) and the diners were

93

weary and sleepy, and the dreary speech had made them unresponsive.

They gave him a round of applause when he stepped up upon the table in front of him—a tribute to his name. Then he began the opening words of that memorable, delightful fancy.

"We haven't all had the good-fortune to be ladies; we haven't all been generals, or poets, or statesmen; but when the toast works down to the babies—we stand on common ground—"

The tired audience had listened in respectful silence through the first half of the sentence. He made one of his effective pauses on the word "babies," and when he added, in that slow, rich measure of his, "we stand on common ground," they let go a storm of applause. There was no weariness and inattention after that. At the end of each sentence, he had to stop to let the tornado roar itself out and sweep by. When he reached the beginning of the final paragraph, "Among the three or four million cradles now rocking in the land are some which this nation would preserve for ages as sacred things if we could know which ones they are," the vast audience waited breathless for his conclusion. Step by step he led toward some unseen climax—some surprise, of course, for that would be his way. Then steadily, and almost without emphasis, he delivered the opening of his final sentence:

"And now in his cradle, somewhere under the flag, the future illustrious commander-in-chief of the American armies is so little burdened with his approaching grandeurs and responsibilities as to be giving his whole strategic mind, at this moment, to trying to find out some way to get his own big toe into his mouth, an achievement which (meaning no disrespect) the illustrious guest of this evening also turned his attention to some fifty-six years ago."

He paused, and the vast crowd had a chill of fear. After all, he seemed likely to overdo it to spoil everything with a cheap joke at the end. No one ever knew better than Mark Twain the value of a pause. He waited now long enough to let the silence become absolute, until the tension was painful, then wheeling to Grant himself he said, with all the dramatic power of which he was master:

"And if the child is but the father of the man, there are mighty few who will doubt that he succeeded!"

94

The house came down with a crash. The linking of their hero's great military triumphs with that earliest of all conquests seemed to them so grand a figure that they went mad with the joy of it. Even Grant's iron serenity broke; he rocked and laughed while the tears streamed down his cheeks.

They swept around the speaker with their congratulations, in their efforts to seize his hand. He was borne up and down the great dining-hall. Grant himself pressed up to make acknowledgments.

"It tore me all to pieces," he said; and Sherman exclaimed, "Lord bless you, my boy! I don't know how you do it!"

The little speech has been in "cold type" so many years since then that the reader of it to-day may find it hard to understand the flame of response it kindled so long ago. But that was another day—and another nation—and Mark Twain, like Robert Ingersoll, knew always his period and his people.

+++++++++++

Mark Twain: Archibald Henderson

Take this little passage, for example, which convulsed one of his London audiences. He was speaking of a high mountain that he had come across in his travels. "It is so cold that people who have been there find it impossible to speak the truth; I know that's a fact (here a pause, a blank stare, a shake of the head, a little stroll across the platform, a sigh, a puff, a smothered groan), because—I've—(another pause)—been—(a longer pause)—there myself."

+++++++++++

Mark Twain – A Biography: Albert Bigelow Paine

Mrs. Clemens and Clara, as often as they had heard him, generally went when the hour of entertainment came: They enjoyed seeing his triumph with the different audiences, watching the effect of his subtle art.

95

One story, the "Golden Arm," had in it a pause, an effective, delicate pause which must be timed to the fraction of a second in order to realize its full value. Somewhere before we have stated that no one better than Mark Twain knew the value of a pause. Mrs. Clemens and Clara were willing to go night after night and hear that tale time and again, for its effect on each new, audience.

++++++++++

Mark Twain – A Biography: Albert Bigelow Paine

And it was either then or on a similar occasion that he replied after this fashion: *I have done more for San Francisco than any other of its old residents. Since I left there it has increased in population fully 300,000. I could have done more—I could have gone earlier—it was suggested.*

Which, by the way, is a perfect example of Mark Twain's humorous manner, the delicately timed pause, and the afterthought. Most humorists would have been contented to end with the statement, "I could have gone earlier." Only Mark Twain could have added that final exquisite touch—"it was suggested."

++++++++++

Autobiography of Mark Twain

I used to play with the pause as other children play with a toy. In my recitals, when I went reading around the world for the benefit of Mr. Webster's creditors, I had three or four pieces in which the pauses performed an important part, and I used to lengthen them or shorten them according to the requirements of the case, and I got much pleasure out of the pause when it was accurately measured, and a certain discomfort when it wasn't.

++++++++++ ++++++++++ ++++++++++

LESSONS: Wait – The Pause

LESSON I: No Word is as Effective as the Rightly Timed Pause.

This is the lesson where I feel I should simply shut up, say nothing and let you hear the sound of silence! And maybe you are thinking "You are right, Conor."

Numerous reviews of Twain's performances reference his uncanny ability to hold audience attention through perfect pausing.

Biographer Albert Bigelow Paine wrote "No one better than Mark Twain knew the value of a pause.... His delivery was a long, monotonous drawl, with the fun invariably coming in at the end of a sentence—after a pause."

The challenge for the speaker is that what technically is very simple—staying quiet—is actually quite difficult. Why? If you are not used to pausing (which sometimes means you looking silently at the audience for three, four, five seconds while the audience which came to hear you speak, is silently looking at you for three, four, five seconds) it can be an unnerving experience. The good news is that the more experience you have of the pause, the easier and more effective it becomes.

LESSON II: Silence Does Speak Volumes

Anyone in a relationship knows that the silent treatment from your partner communicates more than a torrent of words!

Simon and Garfunkel famously sang about The Sound of Silence. Will Rogers allegedly said "Never miss a good chance to shut up." One of the finest cinematic directors and storytellers of the 20th century, Italian maestro Federico Fellini said "If there were a little more silence, if we all kept quiet,... maybe we could understand something."

The message is: Silence can be golden. When you pause, you give your audience time to fully comprehend the message.

When you pause, you give your audience time to absorb and reflect on emotional or profound content.

The pause also works because it has an important psychological effect on the listener. It breaks a pattern they have become used to. It also suggests you are confident and in control.

97

LESSON II: Every Speech Can Benefit from Selective Pausing.

If I was forced to pick one onstage technique to improve the average speaker, it would probably be the deliberate introduction of the planned pause.

When scripting your speech, indicate when and where you will pause. Great speakers do not leave the pause to chance. As Winston Churchill drafted his speeches, he inserted white space to remind him where he should pause. One of the greatest orators of the 20th century planned the pause. Shouldn't you?

Churchill's famous "We shall fight on the beaches" address was powerful, not just because of the compelling text but also because of the wonderful delivery reinforced by simple, short pauses. Here, I illustrate where the defiant Prime Minister paused, albeit briefly, in the final stages of his inspirational speech to the House of Commons on June 4, 1940.

"We shall go on to the end,/ we shall fight in France,/ we shall fight on the seas and oceans, we shall fight/ with growing confidence and growing strength in the air/ we shall defend our Island, whatever the cost may be, we shall fight on the beaches,/ we shall fight on the landing grounds,/ we shall fight in the fields/ and in the streets, we shall fight in the hills,/ we shall never surrender, and if,/ which I do not for a moment believe, this Island or a large part of it were subjugated and starving, then our Empire beyond the seas, armed and guarded by the British Fleet, would carry on the struggle,/ until, in God's good time, the New World, with all its power and might, steps forth to the rescue and the liberation of the old."

When rehearsing, don't just rehearse your words and phrasing. Plan those pauses and rehearse them. Initially every second will feel like an hour – a long hour. But the level of discomfort you feel is a growth experience and will ultimately help you better communicate with your audience.

++++++++++ ++++++++++ ++++++++++

How I Implement all that Learnin'!

Wait – The Pause

The pause is simple – just stay quiet. The pause is hard - it is not easy to stay quiet. On reviewing a number of my speeches, I timed some of my pauses at six to seven seconds. That is an exceptionally long time for a speaker to stay quiet in front of an audience. That is not my norm, but there are times when it is appropriate, as when I have made a profound statement, and I want the audience to really think about it.

Effective pausing is hard and takes experience. I do not recall how I felt when I made my first speeches. I'm sure I was petrified, but it obviously hasn't scarred me! However, as I worked on my speaking expertise and attempted to follow the advice of Twain that "The right word may be effective but no word was ever as effective as a rightly timed pause," I can still remember my discomfort the first few times I deliberately paused, but that initial discomfort now pays dividends.

For instance, when speaking about Brand and Brand Experience I use the following trilogy. It is spoken slowly. After each phrase, I pause for two-three seconds to let the content sink in. As you read it, I ask you to do the same.

Your Behavior creates your Brand/
Your Behavior determines what people say about you/
What people say about you IS your Brand/

Now, let's see how effective you think this trilogy is if there is no pausing. Read the following at normal pace.

Your Behavior creates your Brand, your Behavior determines what people say about you, what people say about you, IS your Brand.

It is a challenge to demonstrate the power of the pause in written material, but I hope you can see the effect.

Note, the effective pausing and delivery for this trilogy was developed over time as I discovered the best way to convey the message that your Behavior creates your Brand.

Rhetorical Question

When I ask a rhetorical question (where I don't necessarily expect a formal response from the audience), I pause.

99

Why? In any environment, when you are asked a question, you need time to respond. Similarly, when I ask my audience a question, the audience needs time to assimilate the question and consider a possible response.

Profound Comment

If I'm about to make a profound or particularly impactful point, I pause before I make the comment. Sometimes I may preface my statement with: "Consider this" (pause) or "Think about the following" (pause). My logic here is that when asking the audience to do something e.g. consider or think, you need to give them time to consider or think.

When they laugh

A common mistake inexperienced speakers make is to stamp on audience laughter. Unlike what TV laughter tracks suggest, the human brain does not react instantaneously to humor. There is a short but definite gap between the punch line and the brain reacting. When you say something you know is funny – wait. When they laugh, leave them laugh! Depending on my audience and the material that generated the laugh, I will sometimes wait even after the laughter is over, and guess what? Someone starts laughing again (not sure why, but it happens) which then ripples through the room.

Note, even today, I sometimes goof and stamp on audience laughter e.g. sometimes, I might ad lib, continue speaking and realize the audience is laughing. But that will happen only once, because the next time I say it, I know the comment is funny and I will wait for the response. It's called experience!

My Process

I will address this further in Narration and Stagecraft, but when drafting my material on paper or laptop, I write—in cap letters--the word PAWS (sic) each place where I intend to keep 'em waiting! Ironic, isn't it that a speaker needs to plan silence!

++++++++++ ++++++++++ ++++++++++

CHAPTER VII

A - Anecdotes and Storytelling

The characters were no creations of my own. I simply sketched them from life. I knew both those boys (Huck Finn and Tom Sawyer) so well that it was easy to write what they did and said.

Mark Twain

VII

*What Mark Twain Learned me 'bout **Anecdotes and Story-**
telling*

◆ Every experience we have provides potential
  for a story

◆ Repackage your stories to suit your audience

◆ Combine and develop characters and incidents

◆ People remember stories better than facts

++++++++++ ++++++++++ ++++++++++

Autobiography of Mark Twain

I confine myself to life with which I am familiar when pre-
tending to portray life. But I confined myself to the boy-life out
on the Mississippi because that had a peculiar charm for me,
and not because I was not familiar with other phases of life.

++++++++++

Mark Twain Speeches: Russian Sufferers

Now, I was going to make a speech—I supposed I was, but
I am not. It is late, late; and so I am going to tell a story; and
there is this advantage about a story, anyway, that whatever
moral or valuable thing you put into a speech, why, it gets
diffused among those involuted sentences, and possibly your
audience goes away without finding out what that valuable
thing was that you were trying to confer upon it; but, dear me,
you put the same jewel into a story and it becomes the key-
stone of that story, and you are bound to get it—it flashes, it
flames, it is the jewel in the toad's head—you don't overlook
that.

++++++++++

103

X Twain sourced much of his material from his own experiences. The following graphically illustrates the point. Excerpt one is from <u>Life on the Mississippi</u>, published in 1883. Excerpt two is from <u>Adventures of Huckleberry Finn</u> published in 1885.

1) *Life on the Mississippi (Twain narrating)*

We struck down through the chute of Island No. 8, and I went below and fell into conversation with a passenger, a handsome man, with easy carriage and an intelligent face. We were approaching Island No. 10, a place so celebrated during the war. This gentleman's home was on the main shore in its neighborhood. I had some talk with him about the war times; but presently the discourse fell upon 'feuds,' for in no part of the South has the vendetta flourished more briskly, or held out longer between warring families, than in this particular region. This gentleman said—

'There's been more than one feud around here, in old times, but I reckon the worst one was between the Darnells and the Watsons. Nobody don't know now what the first quarrel was about, it's so long ago; the Darnells and the Watsons don't know, if there's any of them living, which I don't think there is. Some says it was about a horse or a cow—anyway, it was a little matter; the money in it wasn't of no consequence— none in the world—both families was rich.

The thing could have been fixed up, easy enough; but no, that wouldn't do. Rough words had been passed; and so, nothing but blood could fix it up after that. That horse or cow, whichever it was, cost sixty years of killing and crippling! Every year or so somebody was shot, on one side or the other; and as fast as one generation was laid out, their sons took up the feud and kept it a-going. And it's just as I say; they went on shooting each other, year in and year out—making a kind of a religion of it, you see—till they'd done forgot, long ago, what it was all about. Wherever a Darnell caught a Watson, or a Watson caught a Darnell, one of 'em was going to get hurt—only question was, which of them got the drop on the other. They'd shoot one another down, right in the presence of the family. They didn't hunt for each other, but when they happened to meet, they puffed and begun. Men would shoot boys, boys would shoot men.

A man shot a boy twelve years old—happened on him in the woods, and didn't give him no chance. If he *had* 'a' given him a chance, the boy'd 'a' shot him. Both families belonged to the same church (everybody around here is religious); through all this fifty or sixty years' fuss, both tribes was there every Sunday, to worship.

They lived each side of the line, and the church was at a landing called Compromise. Half the church and half the aisle was in Kentucky, the other half in Tennessee. Sundays you'd see the families drive up, all in their Sunday clothes, men, women, and children, and file up the aisle, and set down, quiet and orderly, one lot on the Tennessee side of the church and the other on the Kentucky side; and the men and boys would lean their guns up against the wall, handy, and then all hands would join in with the prayer and praise; though they say the man next the aisle didn't kneel down, along with the rest of the family; kind of stood guard. I don't know; never was at that church in my life; but I remember that that's what used to be said.

2) Adventures of Huckleberry Finn

Soon as I (Huckleberry Finn) could get Buck down by the corn-cribs under the trees by ourselves, I says:
"Did you want to kill him, Buck?"
"Well, I bet I did."
"What did he do to you?"
"Him? He never done nothing to me."
"Well, then, what did you want to kill him for?"
"Why, nothing—only it's on account of the feud."
"What's a feud?"
"Why, where was you raised? Don't you know what a feud is?"
"Never heard of it before—tell me about it."
"Well," says Buck, "a feud is this way: A man has a quarrel with another man, and kills him; then that other man's brother kills *him*; then the other brothers, on both sides, goes for one another; then the *cousins* chip in—and by and by everybody's killed off, and there ain't no more feud. But it's kind of slow, and takes a long time."
"Has this one been going on long, Buck?"

105

"Well, I should *reckon*! It started thirty year ago, or som'ers along there. There was trouble 'bout something, and then a lawsuit to settle it; and the suit went agin one of the men, and so he up and shot the man that won the suit—which he would naturally do, of course. Anybody would."

"What was the trouble about, Buck?—land?"

"I reckon maybe—I don't know."

"Well, who done the shooting? Was it a Grangerford or a Shepherdson?"

"Laws, how do I know? It was so long ago."

"Don't anybody know?"

"Oh, yes, pa knows, I reckon, and some of the other old people; but they don't know now what the row was about in the first place."

"Has there been many killed, Buck?"

"Yes; right smart chance of funerals. But they don't always kill. Pa's got a few buckshot in him; but he don't mind it 'cuz he don't weigh much, anyway. Bob's been carved up some with a bowie, and Tom's been hurt once or twice."

"Has anybody been killed this year, Buck?"

"Yes; we got one and they got one. 'Bout three months ago my cousin Bud, fourteen year old, was riding through the woods on t'other side of the river, and didn't have no weapon with him, which was blame' foolishness, and in a lonesome place he hears a horse a-coming behind him, and sees old Baldy Shepherdson a-linkin' after him with his gun in his hand and his white hair a-flying in the wind; and 'stead of jumping off and taking to the brush, Bud 'lowed he could out-run him; so they had it, nip and tuck, for five mile or more, the old man a-gaining all the time; so at last Bud seen it warn't any use, so he stopped and faced around so as to have the bullet holes in front, you know, and the old man he rode up and shot him down. But he didn't git much chance to enjoy his luck, for inside of a week our folks laid *him* out."

"I reckon that old man was a coward, Buck."

"I reckon he *warn't* a coward. Not by a blame' sight. There ain't a coward amongst them Shepherdsons—not a one. And there ain't no cowards amongst the Grangerfords either. Why, that old man kep' up his end in a fight one day for half an hour against three Grangerfords, and come out winner. They was all a-horseback; he lit off of his horse and got behind a little

106

woodpile, and kep' his horse before him to stop the bullets; but the Grangerfords stayed on their horses and capered around the old man, and peppered away at him, and he peppered away at them. Him and his horse both went home pretty leaky and crippled, but the Grangerfords had to be *fetched* home—and one of 'em was dead, and another died the next day. No, sir; if a body's out hunting for cowards he don't want to fool away any time amongst them Shepherdsons, becuz they don't breed any of that *kind*."

Next Sunday we all went to church, about three mile, everybody a-horseback. The men took their guns along, so did Buck, and kept them between their knees or stood them handy against the wall. The Shepherdsons done the same. It was pretty ornery preaching—all about brotherly love, and suchlike tiresomeness; but everybody said it was a good sermon, and they all talked it over going home, and had such a powerful lot to say about faith and good works and free grace and preforeordestination, and I don't know that it did seem to me to be one of the roughest Sundays I had run across.

+++++++++

The Adventures of Tom Sawyer

Huck Finn is drawn from life; Tom Sawyer also, but not from an individual—he is a combination of the characteristics of three boys whom I knew, and therefore belongs to the composite order of architecture.

+++++++++

Mark Twain Speeches: Joan of Arc

I was reminded of Jack because I came across a letter to-day which is over thirty years old that Jack wrote. Jack was doomed to consumption. He was very long and slim, poor creature; and in a year or two after he got back from that excursion, to the Holy Land he went on a ride on horseback through Colorado, and he did not last but a year or two.

107

He wrote this letter, not to me, but to a friend of mine; and he said: "I have ridden horseback"—this was three years after—"I have ridden horseback four hundred miles through a desert country where you never see anything but cattle now and then, and now and then a cattle station—ten miles apart, twenty miles apart. Now you tell Clemens that in all that stretch of four hundred miles I have seen only two books—the Bible and (Twain's) *Innocents Abroad*. Tell Clemens the Bible was in a very good condition."

+++++++++++

Mark Twain: How to Tell a Story

I do not claim that I can tell a story as it ought to be told. I only claim to know how a story ought to be told, for I have been almost daily in the company of the most expert story-tellers for many years.

There are several kinds of stories, but only one difficult kind—the humorous. I will talk mainly about that one. The humorous story is American, the comic story is English, the witty story is French. The humorous story depends for its effect upon the manner of the telling; the comic story and the witty story upon the matter.

The humorous story may be spun out to great length, and may wander around as much as it pleases, and arrive nowhere in particular; but the comic and witty stories must be brief and end with a point. The humorous story bubbles gently along, the others burst.

The humorous story is strictly a work of art—high and delicate art—and only an artist can tell it; but no art is necessary in telling the comic and the witty story; anybody can do it. The art of telling a humorous story—understand, I mean by word of mouth, not print—was created in America, and has remained at home.

The humorous story is told gravely; the teller does his best to conceal the fact that he even dimly suspects that there is anything funny about it; but the teller of the comic story tells you beforehand that it is one of the funniest things he has ever heard, then tells it with eager delight, and is the first person to laugh when he gets through. And sometimes, if he has had good success, he is so glad and happy that he will repeat the "nub" of it and glance around from face to face, collecting applause, and then repeat it again. It is a pathetic thing to see.

Very often, of course, the rambling and disjointed humorous story finishes with a nub, point, snapper, or whatever you like to call it. Then the listener must be alert, for in many cases the teller will divert attention from that nub by dropping it in a carefully casual and indifferent way, with the pretence that he does not know it is a nub.

Artemus Ward used that trick a good deal; then when the belated audience presently caught the joke he would look up with innocent surprise, as if wondering what they had found to laugh at. Dan Setchell used it before him, Nye and Riley and others use it to-day.

But the teller of the comic story does not slur the nub; he shouts it at you—every time. And when he prints it, in England, France, Germany, and Italy, he italicizes it, puts some whooping exclamation-points after it, and sometimes explains it in a parenthesis. All of which is very depressing, and makes one want to renounce joking and lead a better life.

++++++++++

Mark Twain Speeches: Missouri University Speech

One night I stole—I mean I removed—a watermelon from a wagon while the owner was attending to another customer. I crawled off to a secluded spot, where I found that it was green. It was the greenest melon in the Mississippi Valley. Then I began to reflect. I began to be sorry. I wondered what George Washington would have done had he been in my place. I thought a long time, and then suddenly felt that strange feeling which comes to a man with a good resolution, and I took up that watermelon and took it back to its owner. I handed him the watermelon and told him to reform. He took my lecture much to heart, and, when he gave me a good one in place of the green melon, I forgave him.

I told him that I would still be a customer of his, and that I cherished no ill-feeling because of the incident—that would remain green in my memory.

ANOTHER VERSION from: *Theoretical Morals*

The first time I ever stole a watermelon; that is, I think it was the first time; anyway, it was right along there somewhere.

I stole it out of a farmer's wagon while he was waiting on another customer. "Stole" is a harsh term. I withdrew—I retired that watermelon. I carried it to a secluded corner of a lumber-yard. I broke it open. It was green. The greenest watermelon raised in the valley that year.

The minute I saw it was green I was sorry, and began to reflect—reflection is the beginning of reform. If you don't reflect when you commit a crime then that crime is of no use; it might just as well have been committed by someone else: You must reflect or the value is lost; you are not vaccinated against committing it again.

I began to reflect. I said to myself: "What ought a boy to do who has stolen a green watermelon? What would George Washington do, the father of his country, the only American who could not tell a lie? What would he do? There is only one right, high, noble thing for any boy to do who has stolen a watermelon of that class: he must make restitution; he must restore that stolen property to its rightful owner." I said I would do it when I made that good resolution. I felt it to be a noble, uplifting obligation. I rose up spiritually stronger and refreshed. I carried that watermelon back—what was left of it—and restored it to the farmer, and made him give me a ripe one in its place.

Now you see that this constant impact of crime upon crime protects you against further commission of crime. It builds you up. A man can't become morally perfect by stealing one or a thousand green watermelons, but every little helps.

++++++++++

Mark Twain Speeches: The Ascot Gold Cup

Once upon a time I went to a public meeting where the oratory of a charitable worker so worked on my feelings that, in common with others, I would have dropped something substantial in the hat—if it had come round at that moment.

The speaker had the power of putting those vivid pictures before one. We were all affected. That was the moment for the hat. I would have put two hundred dollars in. Before he had finished I could have put in four hundred dollars. I felt I could have filled up a blank check—with somebody else's name—and dropped it in.

Well, now, another speaker got up, and in fifteen minutes damped my spirit; and during the speech of the third speaker all my enthusiasm went away. When at last the hat came round I dropped in ten cents—and took out twenty-five.

++++++++++

Mark Twain Speeches: Rogers and Railroads

(To appreciate the following anecdote fully: A "half a crown" in English currency was worth less than 50 cents.)

The chairman says Mr. Rogers is full of practical wisdom, and he is. It is intimated here that he is a very ingenious man, and he is a very competent financier. Maybe he is now, but it was not always so.

I know lots of private things in his life which people don't know, and I know how he started; and it was not a very good start. I could have done better myself. The first time he crossed the Atlantic he had just made the first little strike in oil, and he was so young he did not like to ask questions. He did not like to appear ignorant. To this day he don't like to appear ignorant, but he can look as ignorant as anybody. On board the ship they were betting on the run of the ship, betting a couple of shillings, or half a crown, and they proposed that this youth from the oil regions should bet on the run of the ship. He did not like to ask what a half-crown was, and he didn't know; but rather than be ashamed of himself he did bet half a crown on the run of the ship, and in bed he could not sleep. He wondered if he could afford that outlay in case he lost. He kept wondering over it, and said to himself: "A king's crown must be worth $20,000, so half a crown would cost $10,000." He could not afford to bet away $10,000 on the run of the ship, so he went up to the stakeholder and gave him $150 to let him off.

++++++++++

Mark Twain Speeches: Education and Citizenship

Now I want to tell a story about jumping at conclusions. It was told to me by Bram Stoker, and it concerns a christening. There was a little clergyman who was prone to jump at conclusions sometimes.

One day he was invited to officiate at a christening. He went. There sat the relatives—intelligent-looking relatives they were. The little clergyman's instinct came to him to make a great speech.

He was given to flights of oratory that way—a very dangerous thing, for often the wings which take one into clouds of oratorical enthusiasm are wax and melt up there, and down you come.

But the little clergyman couldn't resist. He took the child in his arms, and, holding it, looked at it a moment. It wasn't much of a child. It was little, like a sweet-potato. Then the little clergyman waited impressively, and then: "I see in your countenances," he said, "disappointment of him. I see you are disappointed with this baby. Why? Because he is so little. My friends, if you had but the power of looking into the future you might see that great things may come of little things. There is the great ocean, holding the navies of the world, which comes from little drops of water no larger than a woman's tears. There are the great constellations in the sky, made up of little bits of stars. Oh, if you could consider his future you might see that he might become the greatest poet of the universe, the greatest warrior the world has ever known, greater than Caesar, than Hannibal, than—er—er" (turning to the father)—"what's his name?"

The father hesitated, then whispered back: "His name? Well, his name is Mary Ann."

++++++++++

Autobiography of Mark Twain

My uncle, John A. Quarles, was a farmer, and his place was in the country four miles from Florida. He had eight children, and fifteen or twenty negroes, and was also fortunate in other ways. Particularly in his character. I have not come

112

across a better man than he was. I was his guest for two or three months every year, from the fourth year after we removed to Hannibal till I was eleven or twelve years old. I have never consciously used him or his wife in a book, but his farm has come very handy to me in literature, once or twice. In "Huck Finn" and in "Tom Sawyer Detective" I moved it down to Arkansas. It was all of six hundred miles, but it was no trouble, it was not a very large farm; five hundred acres, perhaps, but I could have done it if it had been twice as large. And as for the morality of it, I cared nothing for that; I would move a State if the exigencies of literature required it.

++++++++++

Mark Twain Speeches: General Miles and the Dog

I was then under contract for my *Innocents Abroad*, but did not have a cent to live on while I wrote it. So I went to Washington to do a little journalism. There I met an equally poor friend, William Davidson, who had not a single vice, unless you call it a vice in a Scot to love Scotch. Together we devised the first and original newspaper syndicate, selling two letters a week to twelve newspapers and getting $1 a letter. That $24 a week would have been enough for us—if we had not had to support the jug.

But there was a day when we felt that we must have $3 right away—$3 at once. That was how I met the General. It doesn't matter now what we wanted so much money at one time for, but that Scot and I did occasionally want it. The Scot sent me out one day to get it. He had a great belief in Providence, that Scottish friend of mine. He said: "The Lord will provide."

I had given up trying to find the money lying about, and was in a hotel lobby in despair, when I saw a beautiful unfriended dog. The dog saw me, too, and at once we became acquainted. Then General Miles came in, admired the dog, and asked me to price it. I priced it at $3. He offered me an opportunity to reconsider the value of the beautiful animal, but I refused to take more than Providence knew I needed. The General carried the dog to his room.

Then came in a sweet little middle-aged man, who at once began looking around the lobby.

"Did you lose a dog?" I asked. He said he had.

"I think I could find it," I volunteered, "for a small sum."

"'How much?'" he asked. And I told him $3.

He urged me to accept more, but I did not wish to outdo Providence. Then I went to the General's room and asked for the dog back. He was very angry, and wanted to know why I had sold him a dog that did not belong to me.

"That's a singular question to ask me, sir," I replied. "Didn't you ask me to sell him? You started it." And he let me have him. I gave him back his $3 and returned the dog, collect, to its owner.

++++++++++

The Sunday (Portland) Oregonian, 9 August 1895

(Twain's manager for his final lengthy world tour, Major J.B Pond, wrote that this interview with a young reporter was one that the great humorist was particularly happy with and one that best captured his thinking.)

I have always found it rather difficult to choose just the name that suited my ear. 'Tom Sawyer' and 'Huckleberry Finn' were both real characters, but 'Tom Sawyer' was not the real name of the former, nor the name of any person that I ever knew, so far as I can remember, but the name was an ordinary one -- just the sort that seemed to fit the boy, some way, by its sound, and so I used it. No, one doesn't name his characters haphazard..............

Now, 'Arthur Van de Vanter Montague' would have sounded ridiculous, applied to characters like either 'Tom Sawyer' or 'Huck Finn.'"

"Both of those books will always be a well of joy to innumerable boys, Mr. Clemens."

"Well," said Twain, with a smile, "I rather enjoyed writing them. The characters were no creations of my own. I simply sketched them from life. I knew both those boys so well that it was easy to write what they did and said. I've a sort of fondness for 'em anyway.

"I don't believe an author, good, bad, or indifferent, ever lived who created a character. It was always drawn from his recollection of someone he had known. Sometimes, like a composite photograph, an author's presentation of a character may possibly be from the blending of more than two or more real characters in his recollection. But, even when he is making no attempt to draw his character from life, when he is striving to create something different, even then, however ideal his drawing, he is yet unconsciously drawing from memory. It is like a star so far away that the eye cannot discover it through the most powerful telescope, yet if a camera is placed in proper position under that telescope and left for a few hours, a photograph of the star will be the result. So it's the same way with the mind; a character one has known some time in life may have become so deeply buried within the recollection that the lens of the first effort will not bring it to view. But by continued application the author will find, when he is done, that he has etched a likeness of someone he has known before.

"In attempting to represent some character which he cannot recall, which he draws from what he thinks is his imagination, an author may often fall into the error of copying in part a character already drawn by another, a character which impressed itself upon his memory from some book. So he has but made a picture of a picture with all his pains. We mortals can't create, we can only copy. Some copies are good and some are bad."

++++++++++

Autobiography of Mark Twain

(My mother) never used large words, but she had a natural gift for making small ones do effective work. She lived to reach the neighborhood of ninety years, and was capable with her tongue to the last—especially when a meanness or an injustice roused her spirit. She has come handy to me several times in my books, where she figures as Tom Sawyer's "Aunt Polly." I fitted her out with a dialect, and tried to think up other improvements for her, but did not find any. I used Sandy once, also; it was in "Tom Sawyer"; I tried to get him to whitewash the fence, but it did not work. I do not remember what name I called him by in the book.......................

In *Huckleberry Finn* I have drawn Tom Blankenship exactly as he was. He was ignorant, unwashed, insufficiently fed; but he had as good a heart as ever any boy had. His liberties were totally unrestricted. He was the only really independent person--boy or man--in the community, and by consequence he was tranquilly and continuously happy and envied by the rest of us. And as his society was forbidden us by our parents the prohibition trebled and quadrupled its value, and therefore we sought and got more of his society than any other boy's.

++++++++++ ++++++++++ ++++++++++

LESSONS: Anecdotes and Storytelling

LESSON I: Every Experience Provides Potential for a Story.

Mark Twain thought it was well-nigh impossible to create a totally original story. His belief was that all our experiences provide fodder for our stories. In his autobiography, Twain identifies a young waif from Hannibal—Tom Blankenship—as the source for the Huckleberry Finn character. He did contradict this in an interview given to the *Portland Oregonian* in 1895 when he said "Finn was the real name of the other boy, but I tacked on the 'Huckleberry." (Twain's recollection of events was not always consistent, something he never denied.) Irrespective of the origin, it is clear that Huck Finn was drawn from characters Twain knew in his youth.

As a speaker, you can draw from your experiences. Your life is a tapestry of good days, bad days, highs and lows, genuine friends and mean-spirited curmudgeons. You have run the gamut of emotions from A-Z and you have had experiences and challenges which can be of interest to your audience. Of course it is not enough to tell a story. Make a point or provide a lesson learned, a lesson that will benefit your audience.

LESSON II: Repackage Your Stories to Suit your Audience

Your ability to customize your material to different audiences will strongly determine your level of success.

In his later years, Mark Twain told few original stories, but he always had the ability to present his hoary old anecdotes in a fresh and relevant way to his audience.

It is likely, you can provide more than one lesson from your story. The relevance of those lessons will vary depending on your audience. Package your speech to highlight appropriate lessons to your respective audience.

When telling my "Mobile Disco" story, I mention the fact that the police officer had sympathy for me because he realized I was "one more administratively incompetent husband," (I had neglected to put my insurance cert in the car, having been handed it by my wife.) As you can imagine, the "administratively incompetent husband" line has women nodding knowingly and laughing hard (and I think despairing for my wife!)

Do you think I play this line and the concept up when speaking to all you long-suffering wives? You betcha! On the

117

converse side, when I use the "incompetent husband" line to a predominantly male group, I get good (knowing) laughs but I know I will not be able to ham it up as much as I do with the women.

This goes back to "Relate to your audience." When painting pictures with words, it is important that your audience relates to the picture you are painting.

LESSON III: Combine and Develop Characters and Incidents

In the *Oregonian* interview which Twain gave as he started his world tour, the humorist said, "I don't believe an author, good, bad, or indifferent, ever lived who created a character. It was always drawn from his recollection of someone he had known."

Debate continues to rage over the source for the Tom Sawyer character. Some scholars suggest the name was derived from a hard-drinking fireman friend that Twain knew in San Francisco, while Twain at one time suggested the character was based on three boyhood friends. Indeed it is quite possible that there is truth in both references—a combination of boyhood friends named after a character from his adult life.

The debate will never be satisfactorily finalized but there is no doubt that Twain consistently combined, added, developed and exaggerated characters from his life. Tom Sawyer's Aunt Polly is based on Twain's kindly mother while the semi-saintly Sid Sawyer (Tom's younger brother) is based on Twain's adored junior sibling Henry.

LESSON IV: People Remember Stories Better Than Facts

That stories are more powerful and memorable than plain hard facts is a generally accepted truth. But today there is strong scientific evidence to support this contention.

Dr. Paul Zak, of the Center for Neuro-Economics Studies at Claremont Graduate University has studied how stories influence our physiology and behavior. Zak has found that good emotional storytelling releases the hormone oxytocin which helps us to empathize with the storyteller and the characters mentioned. This is why you remember the story you heard at Starbucks three weeks ago but you have very little recollection of the facts and figures mentioned by someone yesterday!

A comment I often hear from coaching clients is "Conor, none of my stories are interesting," to which I respond with subtle Irish charm - "Rubbish!"

Here is one simple exercise for you. Identify some element of your life where you either had an epiphany or a major learning experience. Start writing about that event. Describe the event, the characters, the location. Develop the dialogue that was used by you and the participants. Articulate your emotions at the time. There! You have a story.

One excellent way to enhance your story is to bounce it off participants who were there with you to get their recollection. They may have seen the incident from a different perspective and they will surely recall aspects you have forgotten. If it is not possible to discuss the event with participants, tell your story to friends. Ask for their comments, reactions and suggestions. Write and rewrite the story. Tell and retell. Practice, practice, practice and get honest evaluations. A diamond isn't created overnight, neither is a great, compelling story.

Should your story be factually accurate? The key criteria is that you do not mislead your audience. If presenting a fact based story, be factual, but I have yet to meet a person who does not enhance or exaggerate a story in some way, or if I did, I don't remember the story because I fell asleep while it was being told!

Many excellent speakers have "signature stories" which they "own." You can be sure that the first draft of their signature story is far less interesting, colorful and compelling than what is now being told. Stories do tend to grow as we tell them. (Ask Brian Williams!)

Twain's stories grew. In his autobiography, he writes that a story about "Grandfather's Old Ram" had changed so much since it was published thirty years prior in *Roughing It,* that he had difficulty reading the original version!

Aesop's fables have survived all these years, not because of any facts and figures, but because as Mark Twain understood, stories connect with people. It is a lesson you can implement.

++++++++++ ++++++++++ ++++++++++

How I Implement all that Learnin'!

Anecdotes and Storytelling

This writer has experienced good days, bad days, moments of unbridled joy, dreadful disappointment, pain, angst, happiness, worry, anger, frustration, optimism and a few really bad hangovers! Just like most everyone else.

Many of these experiences feature in my keynotes and presentations. As mentioned previously, the story isn't told just to tell a story. It is told to make a point.

Example: Paying It Forward

To illustrate the power of paying it forward, I recall a simple event that happened after I had been pushed sideways from a job I loved. A few days after "what I thought was the end of my world" a considerate colleague left a potted plant on my desk with the message "Hang in there, Conor. Life is not always fair." I tell my audience that "that simple act of kindness helped me appreciate the impact that simple acts of kindness can have on someone going through tough times. That simple act of kindness motivated me to stay with that organization where I did have a very successful career. (PAWS!) Everyone here has received a 'potted plant,' (PAWS!) a simple act of kindness (PAWS!) which made a difference to you. Everyone here knows someone who can benefit from a 'potted plant,' a simple act of kindness that will put a smile on their face and give them a lift."

The message is effective because the audience hears a story which is easy for them to relate to (who hasn't had disappointments in life?) and where I exhibit vulnerability. As with my "Mobile Disco" anecdote, that story has improved as my pacing, pausing and understanding of potential audience reaction has developed.

Business Storytelling

Marketing, sales, business or insurance professionals spend their day looking at facts and figures, but guess what? Just like everyone else, what they will really remember is a good story, well told, that has a relevant message.

When speaking on topics like leadership, branding, marketing or sales I tell stories from my experiences in Ireland, UK and USA. Although, I have had a successful career, I do not proclaim the wonderful job I did. (My less than sympathetic friends advise that, in any event, it would be a short story!) Instead I explain where I learned from mentors or from mistakes made and lessons learned.

Every product, every brand, every product launch or failure has a story. Those stories are published in Fortune, Forbes, Wall Street Journal, New York Times every day. As with those fun emails you receive, create a database or library of useful material. When you read business biographies, mark the passages that grab your attention. As Louis Pasteur wrote, "Fortune favors the prepared mind."

There is some doubt as to whether Mark Twain actually said "The man who does not read good books has no advantage over the man who can't read them," but there is no doubting the logic of it, for you as a speaker.

Howard Schultz

The best business storyteller I know is Starbucks Chairman and CEO, Howard Schultz who has a masterful ability to communicate messages on branding, leadership and engagement via evocative storytelling. A good investment for you would be *Pour Your Heart Into It* and *Onwards*, two wonderful books by the man who has made charging what some perceive as crazy prices for coffee acceptable, but who understands better than most that he is offering not just coffee, but an experience and a sense of community. I follow Starbucks Investor Relations page to track when Schultz will be speaking, because I believe I will learn from a man who has a superb ability to Relate to his audience via well told Anecdotes and Storytelling.

They say the Irish are great storytellers, but storytelling is an art that takes practice. If I may make so bold, today I tell good, appropriate stories that connect and influence, because I practice, practice, practice telling stories which initially were not always good, appropriate or well told.

Remember Lesson I:

There is no substitute for preparation and practice.

++++++++++ ++++++++++ ++++++++++

121

CHAPTER VIII

I - Involve Inform Inspire

I am but human, and when you, give me a reception like that I am obliged to wait a little while I get my voice. When you appeal to my head, I don't feel it; but when you appeal to my heart, I do feel it.

Mark Twain

VIII

*What Mark Twain Learned me 'bout **Involve, Inform, Inspire***

♦ Use Passion, Pathos and Humor to involve your audience

♦ Tell personal stories

♦ Praise and compliment your audience

++++++++++   ++++++++++ ++++++++++

Following the Equator: Pudd'nhead Wilson's New Calendar

Let us endeavor so to live that when we come to die even the undertaker will be sorry.

++++++++++

Mark Twain Speeches: Books, Authors and Hats

My own history includes an incident which will always connect me with England in a pathetic way, for when I arrived here seven years ago with my wife and my daughter--we had gone around the globe lecturing to raise money to clear off a debt--my wife and one of my daughters started across the ocean to bring to England our eldest daughter. She was twenty four years of age and in the bloom of young womanhood, and we were unsuspecting.

When my wife and daughter—and my wife has passed from this life since—when they had reached mid Atlantic, a cablegram—one of those heartbreaking cablegrams which we all in our days have to experience—was put into my hand. It stated that that daughter of ours had gone to her long sleep. And so, as I say, I cannot always be cheerful, and I cannot always be chaffing; I must sometimes lay the cap and bells aside, and recognize that I am of the human race like the rest, and must have my cares and griefs. And therefore I noticed

125

what Mr. Birrell said—I was so glad to hear him say it—something that was in the nature of these verses here at the top of this:

> "He lit our life with shafts of sun
> And vanquished pain.
> Thus two great nations stand as one
> In honoring Twain."

I am very glad to have those verses. I am very glad and very grateful for what Mr. Birrell said in that connection. I have received since I have been here, in this one week, hundreds of letters from all conditions of people in England--men, women, and children--and there is in them compliment, praise, and, above all and better than all, there is in them a note of affection. Praise is well, compliment is well, but affection—that is the last and final and most precious reward that any man can win, whether by character or achievement, and I am very grateful to have that reward. All these letters make me feel that here in England--as in America--when I stand under the English flag, I am not a stranger. I am not an alien, but at home.

++++++++++

Mark Twain Speeches: Morals and Memories

Now, I recall that when I was a boy I was a good boy—I was a very good boy. Why, I was the best boy in my school. I was the best boy in that little Mississippi town where I lived. The population was only about twenty million. You may not believe it, but I was the best boy in that State—and in the United States, for that matter.

But I don't know why I never heard any one say that but myself. I always recognized it. But even those nearest and dearest to me couldn't seem to see it. My mother, especially, seemed to think there was something wrong with that estimate. And she never got over that prejudice.

Now, when my mother got to be eighty-five years old her memory failed her. She forgot little threads that hold life's patches of meaning together. She was living out West then, and I went on to visit her.

I hadn't seen my mother in a year or so. And when I got there she knew my face; knew I was married; knew I had a family, and that I was living with them. But she couldn't, for the life of her, tell my name or who I was. So I told her I was her boy.

"But you don't live with me," she said.

"No," said I, "I'm living in Rochester."

"What are you doing there?"

"Going to school."

"Large school?"

"Very large."

"All boys?"

"All boys."

"And how do you stand?" said my mother.

"I'm the best boy in that school," I answered.

"Well," said my mother, with a return of her old fire, "I'd like to know what the other boys are like."

++++++++++

Mark Twain Speeches: Votes for Women

Referring to woman's sphere in life, I'll say that woman is always right. For twenty-five years I've been a woman's rights man. I have always believed, long before my mother died, that, with her gray hairs and admirable intellect, perhaps she knew as much as I did. Perhaps she knew as much about voting as I.

I should like to see the time come when women shall help to make the laws. I should like to see that whiplash, the ballot, in the hands of women. As for this city's government, I don't want to say much, except that it is a shame—a shame; but if I should live twenty-five years longer—and there is no reason why I shouldn't—I think I'll see women handle the ballot. If women had the ballot to-day, the state of things in this town would not exist.

If all the women in this town had a vote to-day they would elect a mayor at the next election, and they would rise in their might and change the awful state of things now existing here.

++++++++++

Mark Twain Speeches: Municipal Government

But it is by the laws of the city, it is by the manners of the city, it is by the ideals of the city, it is by the customs of the city and by the municipal government which all these elements correct, support, and foster, by which the foreigner judges the city. It is by these that he realizes that New York may, indeed, hold her head high among the cities of the world. It is by these standards that he knows whether to class the city higher or lower than the other municipalities of the world.

Gentlemen, you have the best municipal government in the world—the purest and the most fragrant. The very angels envy you, and wish they could establish a government like it in heaven. You got it by a noble fidelity to civic duty. You got it by stern and ever-watchful exertion of the great powers with which you are charged by the rights which were handed down to you by your forefathers, by your manly refusal to let base men invade the high places of your government, and by instant retaliation when any public officer has insulted you in the city's name by swerving in the slightest from the upright and full performance of his duty. It is you who have made this city the envy of the cities of the world. God will bless you for it— God will bless you for it. Why, when you approach the final resting-place the angels of heaven will gather at the gates and cry out: "Here they come! Show them to the archangel's box, and turn the limelight on them!"

++++++++++

Mark Twain Speeches: Public Education Association

We believe that out of the public school grows the greatness of a nation. It is curious to reflect how history repeats itself the world over. Why, I remember the same thing was done when I was a boy on the Mississippi River. There was a proposition in a township there to discontinue public schools because they were too expensive. An old farmer spoke up and said if they stopped the schools they would not save anything, because every time a school was closed a jail had to be built.

It's like feeding a dog on his own tail. He'll never get fat. I believe it is better to support schools than jails.

The work of your association is better and shows more wisdom than the Czar of Russia and all his people. This is not much of a compliment, but it's the best I've got in stock.

Yes, you're taught in so many ways. And you're so felicitously taught when you don't know it.

++++++++++

Mark Twain Speeches: The Ladies

The story of the world is adorned with the names of illustrious ones of our own sex—some of them sons of St. Andrew, too—Scott, Bruce, Burns, the warrior Wallace, Ben Nevis—the gifted Ben Lomond, and the great new Scotchman, Ben Disraeli.—[Mr. Benjamin Disraeli, at that time Prime Minister of England, had just been elected Lord Rector of Glasgow University, and had made a speech which gave rise to a world of discussion]—

Out of the great plains of history, tower whole mountain ranges of sublime women: the Queen of Sheba, Josephine, Semiramis, Sairey Gamp; the list is endless—but I will not call the mighty roll, the names rise up in your own memories at the mere suggestion, luminous with the glory of deeds that cannot die, hallowed by the loving worship of the good and the true of all epochs and all climes. Suffice it for our pride and our honor that we in our day have added to it such names as those of Grace Darling and Florence Nightingale.

Woman is all that she should be—gentle, patient, longsuffering, trustful, unselfish, full of generous impulses. It is her blessed mission to comfort the sorrowing, plead for the erring, encourage the faint of purpose, succor the distressed, uplift the fallen, befriend the friendless—in a word, afford the healing of her sympathies and a home in her heart for all the bruised and persecuted children that knock at its hospitable door. And when I say, God bless her, there is none among us who has known the ennobling affection of a wife, or the steadfast devotion of a mother but in his heart will say, Amen!

++++++++++

Mark Twain Speeches: Morals and Memories

When I was seventeen I was very bashful, and a sixteen-year-old girl came to stay a week with us. She was a peach, and I was seized with a happiness not of this world.

One evening my mother suggested that, to entertain her, I take her to the theatre. I didn't really like to, because I was seventeen and sensitive about appearing in the streets with a girl. I couldn't see my way to enjoying my delight in public. But we went.

I didn't feel very happy. I couldn't seem to keep my mind on the play. I became conscious, after a while, that that was due less to my lovely company than my boots. They were sweet to look upon, as smooth as skin, but fitted ten time as close. I got oblivious to the play and the girl and the other people and everything but my boots until—I hitched one partly off. The sensation was sensuously perfect: I couldn't help it. I had to get the other off, partly. Then I was obliged to get them off altogether, except that I kept my feet in the legs so they couldn't get away.

From that time I enjoyed the play. But the first thing I knew the curtain came down, like that, without my notice, and—I hadn't any boots on. What's more, they wouldn't go on. I tugged strenuously. And the people in our row got up and fussed and said things until the peach and I simply had to move on.

We moved—the girl on one arm and the boots under the other.

We walked home that way, sixteen blocks, with a retinue a mile long: Every time we passed a lamp-post, death gripped me at the throat. But we got home—and I had on white socks.

If I live to be nine hundred and ninety-nine years old I don't suppose I could ever forget that walk.

++++++++++

Mark Twain Speeches: Rogers and Railroads

There is one side of Mr. Rogers that has not been mentioned. If you will leave that to me I will touch upon that. There was a note in an editorial in one of the Norfolk papers this morning that touched upon that very thing, that hidden side of Mr. Rogers, where it spoke of Helen Keller and her affection for Mr. Rogers, to whom she dedicated her life book. And she has a right to feel that way, because, without the public knowing anything about it, he rescued, if I may use that term, that marvelous girl, that wonderful Southern girl, that girl who was stone deaf, blind, and dumb from scarlet-fever when she was a baby eighteen months old; and who now is as well and thoroughly educated as any woman on this planet at twenty-nine years of age. She is the most marvelous person of her sex that has existed on this earth since Joan of Arc.

++++++++++

Mark Twain Speeches: Woman's Press Club

As a final instance of the force of limitations in the development of concentration, I must mention that beautiful creature, Helen Keller, whom I have known for these many years. I am filled with the wonder of her knowledge, acquired because shut out from all distraction. If I could have been deaf, dumb, and blind I also might have arrived at something.

++++++++++ ++++++++++ ++++++++++

LESSONS: Involve Inform Inspire

LESSON I: Use Passion, Pathos and Humor to involve your audience

Few will disagree with Mark Twain's comment - "When you appeal to my head, I don't feel it; but when you appeal to my heart, I do feel it."

That the man from Hannibal, Missouri, was a consummate humorist goes without saying, but his unique ability to communicate with his audience often derived from a sense of vulnerability and pain—a vulnerability and pain we all experience as we travel this life.

His emotional writing about the guilt-ridden Huck Finn watching Tom Sawyer's Aunt Sally (see page 38) is superb and surely touches everyone with its pathos—"and see her setting there by her candle in the window with her eyes towards the road and the tears in them; and I wished I could do something for her, but I couldn't, only to swear that I wouldn't never do nothing to grieve her any more. And the third time I waked up at dawn, and slid down, and she was there yet, and her candle was most out, and her old gray head was resting on her hand, and she was asleep."

As discussed previously, your audience has experienced all the emotions you have. Connect with the audience by expressing those emotions.

LESSON II: Tell Personal Stories

It doesn't matter what your speech objective is - inform, persuade, motivate or entertain. You are speaking to human beings--human beings who relate to personal stories. If you can find an opportunity within your speech to present a personal anecdote to reinforce your point of view, use that opportunity. Whether the story is maudlin, humorous, motivational or inspiring will depend on the circumstances, but when told well, it should help you connect, relate and get a visceral, emotional response.

One area where stories can dramatically differentiate a person is at interview. Anyone who has got to the interview stage is there because their resume suggests they can do the job. But when you get there, why will you be remembered over other candidates? A short interesting anecdote will reinforce

132

your candidacy and make you memorable. The result may well be that as the interviewers sit around a table at the end of the day, the decision may well be based on a comment like "Do you remember that candidate who told the story about....?"

LESSON II: Praise and Compliment your Audience

Some years ago, I saw an opening speaker who at the time was a shining star on the speaking circuit. At lunchtime while sitting with a number of other conference delegates, the speaker's performance became a point of discussion. The general consensus was that his speech was "all about me, me, me" and with very little reference to the audience. Today that shining star is not burning very brightly! I am not sure if his lack of connection with the audience is the reason for his fall from the popularity charts, but I took to heart that it is not about the speaker, it is about the audience.

WIIFM (What's in it for me?) is a clichéd but oh-so true mantra to which speakers should pay attention. Unless you are a genuine celebrity, the audience doesn't want to hear about how wonderful you are for forty-five minutes. No. Your audience wants to be recognized and appreciated. Without going over the top and getting soppy, the speaker who praises and compliments the audience will involve and quite possibly inspire them.

As you draft your speech, consider the balance of "I" versus "You" in your speech. Go back to Lesson II – Audience. Do your research. Find some awards, good news, new products and positives about your audience. In your speech, introduce these facts and give the audience a rousing shout out for the wonderful work, results, performance etc. "that YOU have been responsible for."

Providing praise and compliments just two or three times in a forty-five minute speech will have the audience appreciating you. Why? Because you appreciated them.

++++++++++ ++++++++++ ++++++++++

How I Implement all that Learnin'!

Involve – Inform – Inspire

I have mentioned previously that working the room prior to an engagement is my norm. That obviously helps to create a connection, but there is one other simple technique which helps me involve the audience in an effective manner. I learn people's names, so that when I am making my presentation I can point to the back left corner of the room and say something like "I know Maria back there has..." or I may point to the front right and say "As Hank told me before the presentation..."

This simple technique has a number of benefits. It obviously gets the attention of Maria, Hank and their associates. It also again reinforces that "the Irish guy seems to know a lot about us" and finally, I get regular comments like "Conor, your name recall is brilliant!" Believe me, it is not, it is selective and very short term but as Twain said "I love compliments. I love them even when they are not so. My child, I can live on a good compliment two weeks with nothing else to eat."

Many of my clients have get-to-know-you events the night before my speech. I believe it is part of my job and my research to attend these events when invited, even if it means flying in earlier than the keynote might require. These events provide a wonderful opportunity to start that important audience connection and provide a rich source of material that just might get used! A number of clients have jokingly said, "Wow, I need to be careful what I say around you," after I interspersed during the keynote interesting or humorous nuggets picked up the previous night. As of this writing I have not yet been sued for defamation!

Personal Stories

Love her or hate her, Oprah Winfrey proved over many years that she had a unique ability to Involve, Inform and Inspire her audience. Her ability to use passion, pathos and humor to relate to her target audience was beyond compare. The astonishing thing was her ability to get total strangers to tell their personal, often intimate story to a national audience – a national audience that hung on every word. Why? Because

134

everyone loves a good personal story that is full of emotion, happiness, sadness and redemption.

In some keynotes, I tell a story about Rory, a very good schoolboy friend who was shot dead a few years ago. As I recall some of the childhood shenanigans Rory and I got up to, using evocative words and imagery, I feel the audience being drawn in. As I recall that we lost contact in our adult years, but I kept meaning to get back in touch, I see nodding heads from audience members especially when I ask (and pause) "Have you had a similar experience?" For me, this is a story of regret as I never renewed contact with Rory, before he passed away. Even as I write this, I feel sad and annoyed at myself for not having done so, and of course now, I never will.

The story has a clear message and does inspire action. ave Audience members approach me after the keynote to tell me they were inspired to make contact with an old friend. I vividly recall one man say he was going to connect with a sister he had not spoken to in over fifteen years! It is those moments that make a wonderful job even more fulfilling.

If I had simply preached "Stay in touch with old friends," it would have been wallpaper. The personal story is what connected and inspired. As a side note, while discussing the outline of this book with friends, one specifically suggested I reference the "Rory story," which she had heard years previously.

Praise and Compliment

As a two-time cancer survivor (thyroid and prostate), you won't be surprised to know I have quite a few anecdotes and emotions to tell about those little roadblocks! But the essential point I make while telling these stories is that I would not be in a position to write this book "without the care, compassion and kindness of fantastic healthcare professionals like you" and my wonderful family.

While the material about my cancer journeys may sometimes be emotional, it is never maudlin. The anecdotes are interspersed with humor and laughter, as for instance when I state that "having had a thyroidectomy and a prostatectomy, I now have a unique Irish condition known as there is not much left-o-me!"

++++++++++ ++++++++++ ++++++++++

Chapter IX

N - Narration and Stagecraft

He was the most consummate public performer I ever saw, and it was an incomparable pleasure to hear him.

William Dean Howells

IX

*What Mark Twain Learned me 'bout **Narration and Stage-craft***

- ◆ Paint pictures with words
- ◆ Develop a bank of evocative words
- ◆ Practice your stagecraft
- ◆ The speaker "doubles the value of his words" with practiced stagecraft

++++++++++ ++++++++++ ++++++++++

Autobiography of Mark Twain

As I have said, I spent some part of every year at the farm until I was twelve or thirteen years old. The life which I led there with my cousins was full of charm, and so is the memory of it yet. I can call back the solemn twilight and mystery of the deep woods, the earthy smells, the faint odors of the wild flowers, the sheen of rain-washed foliage, the rattling clatter of drops when the wind shook the trees, the far-off hammering of woodpeckers and the muffled drumming of wood-pheasants in the remoteness of the forest, the snap-shot glimpses of disturbed wild creatures scurrying through the grass,—I can call it all back and make it as real as it ever was, and as blessed.

++++++++++

The Chicago Tribune   8 January 1869

Mark Twain (Samuel G. Clemens), is a gentleman of some notoriety, and his effusions are constantly making the rounds of the press. The following sketch will be interesting to those who have not the pleasure of his acquaintance: Blessed with long legs, he is tall, reaching five feet ten inches in his boots; weight, 167 pounds; body lithe and muscular; head round and well set on considerable neck, and feet of no size within the ken of a shoemaker, so he gets his boots and stockings always made to order. Next to Grant he wears the belt for smoking. He smokes tobacco. Drink never crosses the threshold of his humorous mouth. Fun lurks in the corners of it. The eyes are deep set and twinkle like stars in a dark night. The brow overhangs the eyes, and the head is protected from the weather by dark and curling locks. The face is eminently a good one, a laughing face, beaming with humor and genuine good nature. He looks as if he would make a good husband and a jolly father.

As a humorous lecturer, he is a success. There is nothing in his lectures, for he very properly sacrifices everything to make his audience roar, and they do it. His manner is peculiar; he hangs round loose, leaning on the desk, or flirting round the corners of it; then marching and counter-marching in the rear of it, marking off ground by the yard with his tremendous boots. He would laugh at his own jokes, but that his doing so would detract from the fun of his hearers, so he contents himself by refusing to explode, and swallowing his risibility until the lecture is over, when he feels easier, and blows off steam. His voice is a long monotonous drawl, well adapted to his style of speaking. The fun invariably comes in at the end of a sentence, after a pause. When the audience least expects it, some dry remark drops and tickles the ribs, and endangers the waist buttons of the "laughists." During the evening, as if to prove that there was something besides humor in him, he branched out into quite eloquent passages, which were applauded. The lecture was good and the attendance large.

++++++++++

Autobiography of Mark Twain

I can call back the prairie, and its loneliness and peace, and a vast hawk hanging motionless in the sky, with his wings spread wide and the blue of the vault showing through the fringe of their end-feathers. I can see the woods in their autumn dress, the oaks purple, the hickories washed with gold, the maples and the sumacs luminous with crimson fires, and I can hear the rustle made by the fallen leaves as we ploughed through them. I can see the blue clusters of wild grapes hanging amongst the foliage of the saplings, and I remember the taste of them and the smell. I know how the wild blackberries looked, and how they tasted; and the same with the pawpaws, the hazelnuts and the persimmons; and I can feel the thumping rain, upon my head, of hickory-nuts and walnuts when we were out in the frosty dawn to scramble for them with the pigs, and the gusts of wind loosed them and sent them down.

++++++++++

Chicago Tribune 1871

It is plain to see that Twain's success as a platformer results: first, from his being a genuine humorist with audacity and imagination; secondly, from his slow and solemn speech and his sanctimonious bearing and manner. Then the style of his delivery gives all the effect of spontaneity. The jokes are uttered as if he had just thought of them a minute before, and didn't perceive the point of them quite as soon as his audience.

++++++++++

Mark Twain Letter to D. W. Bowser

I notice that you use plain, simple language, short words and brief sentences. That is the way to write English--it is the modern way and the best way. Stick to it; don't let fluff and flowers and verbosity creep in. When you catch an adjective, kill it. No, I don't mean utterly, but kill most of them--then the rest will be valuable. They weaken when they are close together. They give strength when they are wide apart. An adjective habit, or a wordy, diffuse, flowery habit, once fastened upon a person, is as hard to get rid of as any other vice.

++++++++++

Mark Twain: Archibald Henderson

Noah Brooks, editor of the *Alta California*, has written the following graphic piece of description, "Mark Twain's method as a lecturer was distinctly unique and novel. His slow, deliberate drawl, the anxious and perturbed expression of his visage, the apparently painful effort with which he framed his sentences, and, above all, the surprise that spread over his face when the audience roared with delight or rapturously applauded the finer passages of his word-painting, were unlike anything of the kind they had ever known. All this was original; it was Mark Twain.

++++++++++

Autobiography of Mark Twain

I know the stain of blackberries, and how pretty it is; and I know the stain of walnut hulls, and how little it minds soap and water; also what grudged experience it had of either of them. I know the taste of maple sap, and when to gather it, and how to arrange the troughs and the delivery tubes, and how to boil down the juice, and how to hook the sugar after it is made; also how much better hooked sugar tastes than any that is honestly come by, let bigots say what they will. I know how a prize watermelon looks when it is sunning its fat rotundity among pumpkin-vines and "simblins"; I know how to tell when it is ripe without "plugging" it; I know how inviting it looks when it is cooling itself in a tub of water under the bed, waiting; I know how it looks when it lies on the table in the sheltered great floor-space between house and kitchen, and the children gathered for the sacrifice and their mouths watering; I know the crackling sound it makes when the carving-knife enters its end, and I can see the split fly along in front of the blade as the knife cleaves its way to the other end; I can see its halves fall apart and display the rich red meat and the black seeds, and the heart standing up, a luxury fit for the elect; I know how a boy looks, behind a yard-long slice of that melon, and I know how he feels; for I have been there. I know the taste of the watermelon which has been honestly come by,

142

and I know the taste of the watermelon which has been acquired by art. Both taste good, but the experienced know which tastes best.

++++++++++

My Mark Twain: William Dean Howells

It was curious to watch his triumph with the house. His carefully studied effects would reach the first rows in the orchestra first, and ripple in laughter back to the standees against the wall, and then with a fine resurgence come again to the rear orchestra seats, and so rise from gallery to gallery till it fell back, a cataract of applause from the topmost rows of seats. He was such a practiced speaker that he knew all the stops of that simple instrument - man, and there is no doubt that these results were accurately intended from his unerring knowledge.

He was the most consummate public performer I ever saw, and it was an incomparable pleasure to hear him lecture; on the platform he was the great and finished actor which he probably would not have been on the stage.

++++++++++

Mark Twain – A Biography: Albert Bigelow Paine

He did not stand by his chair, as the others had done, but walked over to the Speaker's table, and, turning, faced his audience. I have never seen a more impressive sight than that snow-white figure in that dim-lit, crowded room.

He never touched his notes; he didn't even remember them. He began in that even, quiet, deliberate voice of his, the most even, the most quiet, the most deliberate voice in the world—and, without a break or a hesitation for a word, he delivered a copyright argument, full of humor and serious reasoning, such a speech as no one in that room, I suppose, had ever heard. Certainly it was a fine and dramatic bit of impromptu pleading.

The weary committee (of Congressmen), which had been tortured all day with dull, statistical arguments made by the mechanical device fiends, and dreary platitudes unloaded by men whose chief ambition was to shine as copyright champions, suddenly realized that they were being rewarded for the long waiting. They began to brighten and freshen, and uplift and smile, like flowers that have been wilted by a drought when comes the refreshing shower that means renewed life and vigor. Every listener was as if standing on tiptoe. When the last sentence was spoken the applause came like an explosion.

++++++++++

Mark Twain – A Biography: Albert Bigelow Paine

Whatever his method of beginning, Mark Twain's procedure probably was the purest exemplification of the platform entertainer's art which this country has ever seen. It was the art that makes you forget the artisanship, the art that made each hearer forget that he was not being personally entertained by a new and marvelous friend, who had traveled a long way for his particular benefit. One listener has written that he sat "simmering with laughter" through what he supposed was the continuation of the introduction, waiting for the traditional lecture to begin, when presently the lecturer, with a bow, disappeared, and it was over. The listener looked at his watch; he had been there more than an hour. He thought it could be no more than ten minutes, at most. Many have tried to set down something of the effect his art produced on them, but one may not clearly convey the story of a vanished presence and a silent voice.

++++++++++

Autobiography of Mark Twain

I know the look of green apples and peaches and pears on the trees, and I know how entertaining they are when they are inside of a person. I know how ripe ones look when they are piled in pyramids under the trees, and how pretty they are and how vivid their colors. I know how a frozen apple looks, in a barrel down cellar in the winter-time, and how hard it is to bite, and how the frost makes the teeth ache, and yet how good it is, notwithstanding. I know the disposition of elderly people to select the specked apples for the children, and I once knew ways to beat the game. I know the look of an apple that is roasting and sizzling on a hearth on a winter's evening, and I know the comfort that comes of eating it hot, along with some sugar and a drench of cream. I know the delicate art and mystery of so cracking hickory-nuts and walnuts on a flatiron with a hammer that the kernels will be delivered whole, and I know how the nuts, taken in conjunction with winter apples, cider and doughnuts, make old people's tales and old jokes sound fresh and crisp and enchanting, and juggle an evening away before you know what went with the time.

++++++++++

Mark Twain Speeches: Mark Twain's First Appearance

On October 5, 1906, Mr. Clemens, following a musical recital by his daughter in Norfolk, Connecticut, addressed her audience on the subject of stage-fright. He thanked the people for making things as easy as possible for his daughter's American debut as a contralto, and then told of his first experience before the public:-

My heart goes out in sympathy to anyone who is making his first appearance before an audience of human beings. By a direct process of memory I go back forty years, less one month—for I'm older than I look.

I recall the occasion of my first appearance. San Francisco knew me then only as a reporter, and I was to make my bow to San Francisco as a lecturer. I knew that nothing short of compulsion would get me to the theatre. So I bound myself by a hard-and-fast contract so that I could not escape. I got to the theatre forty-five minutes before the hour set for the lecture. My knees were shaking so that I didn't know whether I could stand up. If there is an awful, horrible malady in the world, it is stage-fright-and seasickness. They are a pair. I had stage-fright then for the first and last time. I was only seasick once, too. It was on a little ship on which there were two hundred

145

other passengers. I—was—sick. I was so sick that there wasn't any left for those other two hundred passengers.

It was dark and lonely behind the scenes in that theatre, and I peeked through the little peek holes they have in theatre curtains and looked into the big auditorium. That was dark and empty, too. By-and-by it lighted up, and the audience began to arrive.

I had got a number of friends of mine, stalwart men, to sprinkle themselves through the audience armed with big clubs. Every time I said anything they could possibly guess I intended to be funny they were to pound those clubs on the floor. Then there was a kind lady in a box up there, also a good friend of mine, the wife of the Governor. She was to watch me intently, and whenever I glanced toward her she was going to deliver a gubernatorial laugh that would lead the whole audience into applause.

At last I began. I had the manuscript tucked under a United States flag in front of me where I could get at it in case of need. But I managed to get started without it. I walked up and down—I was young in those days and needed the exercise—and talked and talked.

Right in the middle of the speech I had placed a gem. I had put in a moving, pathetic part which was to get at the hearts and souls of my hearers. When I delivered it they did just what I hoped and expected. They sat silent and awed. I had touched them. Then I happened to glance up at the box where the Governor's wife was—you know what happened.

Well, after the first agonizing five minutes, my stage-fright left me, never to return. I know if I was going to be hanged I could get up and make a good showing, and I intend to. But I shall never forget my feelings before the agony left me, and I got up here to thank you for her for helping my daughter, by your kindness, to live through her first appearance. And I want to thank you for your appreciation of her singing, which is, by-the-way, hereditary.

+++++++++

My Mark Twain: William Dean Howells

We had a peculiar pleasure in looking off from the high windows on the pretty Hartford landscape, and down from them into the tops of the trees clothing the hillside by which his house stood. We agreed that there was a novel charm in trees seen from such a vantage, far surpassing that of the farther scenery. He had not been a country boy for nothing; rather he had been a country boy, or, still better, a village boy, for everything that Nature can offer the young of our species, and no aspect of her was lost on him. We were natives of the same vast Mississippi Valley; and Missouri was not so far from Ohio but that we were akin in our first knowledges of woods and fields as we were in our early parlance. I had outgrown the use of mine through my greater bookishness, but I gladly recognized the phrases which he employed for their lasting juiciness and the long-remembered savor they had on his mental palate....

He was, beyond any author I have known, without favorite phrases or pet words. He utterly despised the avoidance of repetitions out of fear of tautology. If a word served his turn better than a substitute, he would use it as many times in a page as he chose.

++++++++++

The Life of Brett Harte: Henry Childs Merwin

(Twain) spoke in a slow, rather satirical drawl, which was in itself irresistible. He went on to tell one of those extravagant stories, and half unconsciously dropped into the lazy tone and manner of the original narrator. I asked him to tell it again to a friend who came in, and then asked him to write it out for *The Californian*. He did so, and when published it was an emphatic success. It was the first work of his that had attracted general attention, and it crossed the Sierras for an Eastern reading. The story was *The Jumping Frog of Calaveras*. It is now known and laughed over, I suppose, wherever the English language is spoken; but it will never be as funny to any one in print as it was to me, told for the first time by the unknown Twain himself on that morning in the San Francisco Mint.

++++++++++

Mark Twain Speeches: The Savage Club

I am not one of those who in expressing opinions confine themselves to facts. I don't know anything that mars good literature so completely as too much truth. Facts contain a deal of poetry, but you can't use too many of them without damaging your literature.

++++++++++

My Mark Twain: William Dean Howells

What we have strongly conceived we ought to make others strongly imagine, and we ought to use every genuine art to that end.

++++++++++

Following the Equator: Pudd'nhead Wilson's New Calendar

As to the Adjective: When in doubt, strike it out.

++++++++++

Autobiography of Mark Twain

I know the look of Uncle Dan'l's kitchen as it was on privileged nights when I was a child, and I can see the white and black children grouped on the hearth, with the firelight playing on their faces and the shadows flickering upon the walls, clear back toward the cavernous gloom of the rear, and I can hear Uncle Dan'l telling the immortal tales which Uncle Remus Harris was to gather into his books and charm the world with, by and by; and I can feel again the creepy joy which quivered through me when the time for the ghost-story of the "Golden Arm" was reached—and the sense of regret, too, which came over me, for it was always the last story of the evening, and there was nothing between it and the unwelcome bed.

++++++++++

Mark Twain Speeches: Rogers and Railroads

That is not all Mr. Rogers has done; but you never see that side of his character, because it is never protruding; but he lends a helping hand daily out of that generous heart of his. You never hear of it. He is supposed to be a moon which has one side dark and the other bright. But the other side, though you don't see it, is not dark; it is bright, and its rays penetrate, and others do see it who are not God.

I would take this opportunity to tell something that I have never been allowed to tell by Mr. Rogers, either by my mouth or in print, and if I don't look at him I can tell it now.

In 1893, when the publishing company of Charles L. Webster, of which I was financial agent, failed, it left me heavily in debt. If you will remember what commerce was at that time you will recall that you could not sell anything, and could not buy anything, and I was on my back; my books were not worth anything at all, and I could not give away my copyrights. Mr. Rogers had long enough vision ahead to say, "Your books have supported you before, and after the panic is over they will support you again," and that was a correct proposition. He saved my copyrights, and saved me from financial ruin. He it was who arranged with my creditors to allow me to roam the face of the earth for four years and persecute the nations thereof with lectures, promising that at the end of four years I would pay dollar for dollar. That arrangement was made; otherwise I would now be living out-of-doors under an umbrella, and a borrowed one at that.

You see his white mustache and his head trying to get white (he is always trying to look like me—I don't blame him for that). These are only emblematic of his character, and that is all.

++++++++++

Autobiography of Mark Twain

I can remember the bare wooden stairway in my uncle's house, and the turn to the left above the landing, and the rafters and the slanting roof over my bed, and the squares of moonlight on the floor, and the white cold world of snow outside, seen through the curtainless window. I can remember the howling of the wind and the quaking of the house on stormy nights, and how snug and cozy one felt, under the blankets, listening, and how the powdery snow used to sift in, around the sashes, and lie in little ridges on the floor, and make the place look chilly in the morning, and curb the wild desire to get up—in case there was any. I can remember how very dark that room was, in the dark of the moon, and how packed it was with ghostly stillness when one woke up by accident away in the night, and forgotten sins came flocking out of the secret chambers of the memory and wanted a hearing; and how ill-chosen the time seemed for this kind of business; and how dismal was the hoo-hooing of the owl and the wailing of the wolf, sent mourning by on the night wind.

I remember the raging of the rain on that roof, summer nights, and how pleasant it was to lie and listen to it, and enjoy the white splendor of the lightning and the majestic booming and crashing of the thunder. It was a very satisfactory room; and there was a lightning-rod which was reachable from the window, an adorable and skittish thing to climb up and down, summer nights, when there were duties on hand of a sort to make privacy desirable.

++++++++++

Mark Twain Speeches: The Old Fashioned Printer

The chairman's historical reminiscences of Gutenberg have caused me to fall into reminiscences, for I myself am something of an antiquity. All things change in the procession of years, and it may be that I am among strangers. It may be that the printer of to-day is not the printer of thirty-five years ago. I was no stranger to him. I knew him well. I built his fire for him in the winter mornings; I brought his water from the village pump; I swept out his office; I picked up his type from under his stand; and, if he were there to see, I put the good type in his case and the broken ones among the "hell matter"; and if he wasn't there to see, I dumped it all with the "pi" on the imposing-stone—for that was the furtive fashion of the cub, and I was a cub. I wetted down the paper Saturdays, I turned it Sundays—for this was a country weekly; I rolled, I washed the rollers, I washed the forms, I folded the papers, I carried them around at dawn Thursday mornings. The carrier was then an object of interest to all the dogs in town. If I had saved up all the bites I ever received, I could keep M. Pasteur busy for a year.

++++++++++

Mark Twain – A Biography: Albert Bigelow Paine

The inimitable Mark Twain, delivered himself last night of his first lecture on the Sandwich Islands, or anything else.

"Some time before the hour appointed to open his head the Academy of Music (on Pine Street) was densely crowded with one of the most fashionable audiences it was ever my privilege to witness during my long residence in this city. The Elite of the town were there, and so was the Governor of the State, occupying one of the boxes, whose rotund face was suffused with a halo of mirth during the whole entertainment. The audience promptly notified Mark by the usual sign—stamping—that the auspicious hour had arrived, and presently the lecturer came sidling and swinging out from the left of the stage. His very manner produced a generally vociferous laugh from the assemblage. He opened with an apology, by saying that he had partly succeeded in obtaining a band, but at the last moment the party engaged backed out. He explained that he had hired a man to play the trombone, but he, on learning that he was the only person engaged, came at the last moment and informed him that he could not play. This placed Mark in a bad predicament, and wishing to know his reasons for deserting him at that critical moment, he replied, 'That he wasn't going to make a fool of himself by sitting up there on the stage and blowing his horn all by himself.' After the applause sub-sided, he assumed a very grave countenance and commenced his remarks proper with the following well-known sentence: 'When, in the course of human events,' etc. He lectured fully an hour and a quarter, and his humorous sayings were inter-spersed with geographical, agricultural, and statistical re-marks, sometimes branching off and reaching beyond, soar-ing, in the very choicest language, up to the very pinnacle of descriptive power.

++++++++++

The Chicago Evening Post, 19 December 1871

The entertainment of the season, thus far, was the curious, disjointed, delightful talk of Mark Twain (Clemens is his mar-ried name), last evening, in the Michigan Avenue Baptist Church, below Twenty-second Street.

Every seat in the house, four hundred chairs in the aisles, and standing-room for two or three hundred, were crowded full, when the lank, lantern-jawed, and impudent Californian bestrode the stage as if it were the deck of a steam-boat, and, getting to the middle of the front, rubbed his bony hands, and gazed around. A thin man of five feet ten, thirty-five, or so, eyes that penetrate like a new gimlet, nasal prow projected and pen-dulous, carrotty, curly hair, and mustache, arms that are al-ways in the way, expression dreadfully melancholy, he stares inquisitively here and there, and cranes his long neck around the house like a bereaved Vermonter who has just come from the death-bed of his mother-in-law, and is looking for a sexton. For something like a minute, he says not a word, but rubs his hands awkwardly, and continues the search. Finally, just as the spectators are about to break into giggles, he opens his capacious mouth, and begins in a slow drawl,--about three words a minute by the watch.

Mr. Twain took his auditors on a flying trip to California and the mountain mining-regions; giving alternate glimpses of sense and nonsense, of humor, burlesque, sentiment, and sat-ire that kept the audience in the most sympathetic mood. He dipped into pathos, rose into eloquence, kept sledding right along in a fascinating nasal snarl, looking and speaking like an embarrassed deacon telling his experience, and punctuating his tardy fun with the most complicated awkwardness of gesture. Now he snapped his fingers; now he rubbed his hands softly, like the catcher of the champion nine; now he caressed his left palm with his dexter fingers, like the end minstrel-man propounding a conundrum; now he put his arms akimbo, like a disgusted auctioneer; and now he churned the air in the vicinity of his imperiled head with his outspread hands, as if he was fighting mosquitoes at Rye Beach. Once he got his arms tangled so badly, that three surgeons were seen to edge their way quietly toward the stage, expecting to be summoned; but he unwound himself during the next anecdote.

++++++++++

Mark Twain Speeches: The Weather

If we hadn't our bewitching autumn foliage, we should still have to credit the weather with one feature which compensates for all its bullying vagaries—the ice-storm: when a leafless tree is clothed with ice from the bottom to the top—ice that is as bright and clear as crystal; when every bough and twig is strung with ice-beads, frozen dew-drops, and the whole tree sparkles cold and white, like the Shah of Persia's diamond plume. Then the wind waves the branches and the sun comes out and turns all those myriads of beads and drops to prisms that glow and burn and flash with all manner of colored fires, which change and change again with inconceivable rapidity from blue to red, from red to green, and green to gold—the tree becomes a spraying fountain, a very explosion of dazzling jewels; and it stands there the acme, the climax, the supremest possibility in art or nature, of bewildering, intoxicating, intolerable magnificence. One cannot make the words too strong.

++++++++++

Autobiography of Mark Twain

I remember the pigeon seasons, when the birds would come in millions, and cover the trees, and by their weight break down the branches. They were clubbed to death with sticks; guns were not necessary, and were not used. I remember the squirrel hunts, and the prairie-chicken hunts, and the wild-turkey hunts, and all that; and how we turned out, mornings, while it was still dark, to go on these expeditions, and how chilly and dismal it was, and how often I regretted that I was well enough to go. A toot on a tin horn brought twice as many dogs as were needed, and in their happiness they raced and scampered about, and knocked small people down, and made no end of unnecessary noise. At the word, they vanished away toward the woods, and we drifted silently after them in the melancholy gloom. But presently the gray dawn stole over the world, the birds piped up, then the sun rose and poured light and comfort all around, everything was fresh and dewy and fragrant, and life was a boon again. After three hours of tramping we arrived back wholesomely tired, overladen with game, very hungry, and just in time for breakfast.

++++++++++

The Seattle Post-Intelligencer, 14 August 1895

There is but one Mark Twain. He is not classic, and he is just as far from being conventional; but people like him and listen to him all the more because he is himself. Last night at the Seattle theater a crowded audience heard him for an hour and a half with unwearying enjoyment as he gave one of those strange medleys of humor and philosophy which have so much the sound of a great literary improvisation. To tell the story of such a lecture is like trying to narrate a laugh. Those who heard it enjoyed it, and those who did not cannot conceive of it.

The string on which the great humorist strung the many anecdotes and jests that made up the body of the evening's entertainment was a pretended moral lecture, which he said he had in mind to work out at his leisure. Thus he would tell some droll story and draw therefrom some far-fetched moral, which found its chief pith and merit in being far-fetched. The following will serve as a poor sample of a dozen of its kind:

"When I was a boy my father lived in a little Missouri village on the banks of the Mississippi river. The place was so small that it was necessary for one man to hold several such offices as coroner, mayor, postmaster, in order to maintain the dignity of each. My father was the incumbent. He had a small office built wherein his numerous functions were discharged. It was not often that he got to act as coroner, but now and then the community furnished a corpse. In the office was a sofa, which was to me a very useful article of furniture. We boys were told not to go fishing. For that reason we went. On returning from one of these excursions, I did not care to go at once into the home circle. I preferred letting the home atmosphere cool down till next morning. Accordingly I would creep into that office and use that sofa as a bed.

"One day there had been a fight in the village while I was out fishing. One man had killed another with a bowie knife. The corpse had been stripped to the waist and laid out on the floor of the little office ready for the inquest next morning. Late at night I came in, ignorant of what had occurred. I crept to the sofa was just sinking into the deep, sweet sleep which is the reward of honest toil when a strange feeling came over me as I thought I saw some uncanny object on the floor. I first resolve to feel it, but concluded I would wait. Just beyond it were some squares of moonlight on the floor and I decided to wait till the moonlight crept along to where the thing lay. Only those who have waited for the moon at midnight know how slow it is. At last there lay a pallid human hand in the ghostly light. I tried to turn over and count a thousand till the moon should reveal what I knew now was there, but I got no further than seventy-five. After what seemed an interminable time the white, muscular arm, then the rigid, set face, then the body with the knife wound on the left side came into view. I went away from there. I do not mean to imply that I left hurriedly. I simply went. I went through the window. I took the sash along with me. I did not have any special use for the sash, but under the circumstances it was easier to take it than it was to leave it.

"Now, in planning my great lecture on morals, I mean to introduce this story to illustrate the principle that early in life a young man should certainly gauge his limitations. He should know just exactly how brave he is, how far he can rely on his own courage before he is compelled to begin to use his discretion."

In similar vein the lecturer gave the story of the bucking horse from his "Roughing It," which he said he proposed to use in his great lecture "to show that we should be careful how we make the acquaintance of strangers." Then he shot off at a merry tangent to say that Mount Ranier had been pursuing this policy toward him during his first visit. To illustrate the moral that conclusions must not be drawn hastily, the gave the story of the preacher's long baptismal harangue over what he supposed to be a boy baby, till the name of Mary Ann was announced. In much the same tone followed the story of the grandfather and the ram, and of Jim and Huckleberry Finn when these two worthies were running away, and of "My first theft."

Leaving this hypothetical lecture on morals, Mr. Clemens was proceeding to give the substance of his famous essay on the German language, when a rough voice from the gallery cried out: "Haf you been to Heidelberg?" "Yes," retorted the lecturer, with ready wit; "I studied German there and I learned many other things there also, among them how to drink beer." The questioner subsided.

As a conclusion, Mr. Clemens gave his famous ghost story. It was the strongest piece given by him, or rather, he gave it most strongly, and when the unexpected denouement was reached there was many a sudden jump among those who had been betrayed into breathless expectancy through the weird magic of the well-told dialect story.

As a mark of honor Mr. Clemens was called before the curtain, and in response he gave "The Stammerer" in mirth-provoking style.

++++++++++ ++++++++++ ++++++++++

LESSONS: Narration and Stagecraft

LESSON I: Paint Pictures with Words

When Mark Twain goes into descriptive mode, you "see" what he sees, you "hear" what he hears. In his autobiography, you are there with him as he describes "the earthy smells, the faint odors of the wild flowers, the sheen of rain-washed foliage, the rattling clatter of drops when the wind shook the trees, the far-off hammering of woodpeckers and the muffled drumming of wood-pheasants in the remoteness of the forest." Painting pictures with words!

The ability to describe a scene in such vivid detail that your audience can see it, can feel it, can almost smell and touch it, is partly a gift, but is generally the result of painstaking development, writing and rewriting. When you as a speaker get it right, when you articulate in a nuanced, paced manner, you will connect in a visceral way with your audience.

The magic of this concept is that everyone will see the picture in their mind differently, but in a way that is drawn from that person's experience. The thrill for you is when someone says "I could see it. It was almost as if I was there."

LESSON II: Develop a Bank of Evocative Words

One word can change the meaning of a sentence and the perception of the listener. If memory serves me right, I first saw a version of this exercise in a book by screenwriter William Goldman. In this exercise, pause for a moment after reading each of the sentences about Carlos. You will picture some quite different scenarios even though only one word changes.

Carlos sauntered into the hospital.

Carlos ran into the hospital.

Carlos scurried into the hospital.

Carlos plodded into the hospital.

What if the name changes? Forgive the possible stereotyping here but do you picture a different individual if instead of Carlos, I mention Rajeev, Paddy, Jean-Pierre, Gwendolyn, Hans, Hamish?

One word can change a sentence and the meaning of what you say. Learn from the master and choose your words carefully. Twain added life to his communication with well chosen, evocative material.

"Nearby is an interesting ruin—the MEAGRE remains of an ancient HEATHEN temple." (*Roughing It*)

"The crowd SWARMED ashore and soon the forest distances and CRAGGY heights echoed far and near with shoutings and laughter." (*Tom Sawyer*)

"The falls rise in a seven-stepped stairway of FOAMY and GLITTERING cascades, and make a picture which is as charming as it is unusual." (*A Tramp Abroad*)

Here's a simple exercise:

Develop your bank of evocative words. As you see or hear a word that strikes you, write it down and file it away for future use. Developing a bank of evocative words means you are constantly improving your skill set and knowledge base. Ultimately, it will make a difference to the quality of your presentations.

LESSON III: The Speaker "Doubles the value of his words" with Practiced Stagecraft

Mark Twain believed that the written word was quite different to the verbal presentation. "Spoken speech is one thing, written speech is quite another," he said in a 1901 interview," and also believed that the "author (on stage) doubles the value of his words," through movement, pacing, pausing and generally good stagecraft.

But while stagecraft may be natural to a few, the vast majority of speakers grow and develop through getting out there on stage and learning as Twain said "secrets not to be got out of books, but only acquirable by experience."

Toastmasters is a wonderful environment to learn some speech basics, but choose a club where you will get good, insightful evaluations.

Practice your speechmaking at Rotary and Kiwanis. Most Rotary clubs seek a speaker every week of every month of every year! That is a lot of opportunity to practice a fifteen minute speech and develop a stage presence. Go do it!

++++++++++ ++++++++++ ++++++++++

How I Implement all that Learnin'!

Narration and Stagecraft

Toastmasters

Many in the professional speaking business express surprise that I am a member of Toastmasters. However, if you ever get a chance to visit Windy City Professional Speakers, long overseen by the inestimable Stan Piskorski, you will understand why. At Windy City, we present our material, normally in ten-fifteen minute modules to a member audience that consists of professional speakers, trainers, speechwriters etc. Then the fun starts! The speaker sits down, shuts up (mandatory) and receives round robin evaluations in an encouraging format but most definitely not uncritical. (I will show you my scars sometime.) The vast majority of guests who attend express an interest in joining (they have to audition), but we have had more than a few who say "Oh, Oh! This ain't for me."

Whatever expertise I have developed as a speaker has occurred because I work extremely hard at my craft, pay very careful attention to evaluations—especially of new material, and regularly practice my material in front of people who will not give me an easy evaluation.

You won't be surprised to know that *What Mark Twain Learned Me 'bout Public Speakin'* is offered as a workshop and seminar to corporate and association clients. While developing the content for the program, the individual lessons (five to seven minute modules) were presented numerous times to Toastmasters who have not been afraid to take me to task on the clarity and efficacy of my message and examples.

I regularly compete in Toastmasters speech competitions and have been lucky enough to win Chicago (240+ clubs) three times. The most recent victory brought me to Kuala Lumpur for the world semi-finals where better stories sent me packing for the seventeen hour return journey to Chicago! However, the "luck" happened thanks to constant practice, rehearsal, rewriting and rehearsing of five-seven minute speeches. Fellow professional speaker Vickie Austin constantly states "The harder you work, the luckier you get." Ain't that the truth!

My modules are now regularly inserted into my keynote presentations. The aforementioned "Rory story" was developed and polished for Toastmasters competition. A yarn I created to win Chicago Humorous Speaker of the Year titled *Customer Service in San Quentin Prison!* (yup, you read it right!) is now a humorous interlude in my programs on customer service.

Toastmasters is not for everyone, but if you find a club where you get good, critical evaluations and the opportunity to practice, practice, practice for an amazingly inexpensive cost, it is a no brainer.

My Speechwriting process

Over the course of this book, I provide an overview of my writing and speech development process. I hope Mark Twain would approve of my process.

Let's assume that I am preparing a keynote for my widget client on *Creating a Top o' the Morning Customer Experience through The Gift of GAB* (Goals, Attitude, Behavior)

At this stage, I do not need to draft the speech in full because I have the core framework. However, what you will see a few days before the presentation is a document that starts with speech objective, then an outline of the various lessons, anecdotes, quips, quotes and support material for GAB. The transitions, anecdotes and examples specific to my widget client are drafted carefully.

The outline is then color coded to show Serious Message (red), Humorous Anecdote (green) and Pathos (blue). I will also highlight pausing and pacing. I am playing the role of a music composer, in a sense scoring my speech. This helps me get a good feel for the speech flow and ensures there is an effective balance and rhythm to the program.

The peroration which should bring the keynote to an inspiring, crescendo-like conclusion gets written out in full. This may only be three hundred words, but when done correctly and customized to my client, these are the words that will have the audience leaving with a smile on the face, a beat in the heart (always important!), a spring in the step and memorable inspirational ideas to take back to the workplace.

A good speech is akin to a Bruce Springsteen concert. The Boss has an uncanny ability to play to, and with his audience. The great rocker's concerts showcase numerous emotions and are full of energy. Sometimes it is physical energy, sometimes emotional energy, sometimes intellectual energy. Sometimes he goes at one hundred miles an hour and sometimes he pauses... takes it slowly, tells a humorous or poignant anec-dote, then... the pace picks up and picks up and picks up until you are now again, going more than one hundred miles an hour, and you wonder how a man well into his sixties can have so much energy and connect so well with so many people.

But even Springsteen had some learnin' to do! Legendary music impresario Clive Davis once told the young Bruce he needed to work the stage better and put more energy into his performance. At that time, the Boss was not the master of his craft that he is today. But the man from New Jersey played anywhere and everywhere he could, constantly writing, rewrit-ing and improvising, eventually becoming famous for his four hour shows (which he claims he rarely ever did!)

Springsteen writes a set list for every concert. (When tour-ing Scandinavia in 2013, he played fifty-eight different songs over three nights!) Scripting my outline, deciding on the exam-ples and stories to tell is my equivalent of a set list, a set list which can and does change depending on audience reaction.

Words Words Words

Heralded *New York Times* Columnist William Safire (1929-2009) was a linguaphile—a lover of language—who for thirty years wrote a weekly column *On Language* for that esteemed publication. His magnificent tome *Lend Me Your Ears: Great Speeches in History* should be on every speakers bookshelf.

Safire was also a speechwriter for Richard Nixon, so you are probably thinking, "Well he can't have been that good a writer," as Nixon will never go down in presidential annals as a great speaker. Nixon had such faith in Safire that the Presi-dent asked him to prepare a speech in the event that the first moon landing proved to be a disaster!

Nixon had other wonderful writers on his staff. His prob-lem was he had no idea how to use the words he was given. Great words do not make great speeches. Great speeches need great words, (sometimes) great events, great stagecraft and voice projection.

Albert Mehrabian, Professor Emeritus of Psychology at UCLA is widely quoted for his study on verbal and non-verbal communication which suggests that there are three elements to communication – words (7%), voice tone (38%), body language (55%). The good professor rails about how his study (which was primarily on feelings and attitudes) has been taken out of context and is not relevant to all communication. However, there is little doubt that the impact you make with your audience will depend not just on your words but on your stage-craft, movement, voice projection, eye-contact and the passion you bring to the event. A good message is essential. How you present that good message is what will determine whether your audience says "That speaker was good."

Today's Evocative Word

One of my daily tweets @IrishmanSpeaks relates to "Today's evocative word to keep 'em evocatin'!" More and more, I am using words from Mark Twain's body of work. Not all the words I tweet enter my keynotes, but a recent seven day list of evocative words consisted of:

Luminous (The Prince and the Pauper)
Pervading (Following the Equator)
Brooding (The Adventures of Tom Sawyer)
Freckled (The Adventures of Tom Sawyer)
Cloistered (A Tramp Abroad)
Loathsome (The Gilded Age)
Portly – (Innocents Abroad)

In the past three days, words I have dropped into my "Evocative file" include "Placid," "Lurking" and "Quaint." When will I use them? Who knows, but it is new deposits to a bank of resources that gets continuously enriched.

My genuine hope is that whether you are speaking to ten or ten thousand, whether you want to get 'em laughing or learning, the MARK TWAIN acronym provides a solid, fun and unique framework to help you succeed.

Our favorite author said "Eloquence is the essential thing in a speech, not information." I hope you have received information that will help you add eloquence. And if that hasn't happened, well....!

"All you need in this life is ignorance and confidence, and then success is sure." – Mark Twain Notebook, 1887

++++++++++ ++++++++++ ++++++++++

IT IS NOBLE TO TEACH ONESELF, BUT STILL NOBLER TO TEACH OTHERS--AND LESS TROUBLE.

Mark Twain - Doctor Van Dyke speech, 1906

Huge THANKS to Mark Anderson for the wonderful original illustrations.

About the Author

Conor Cunneen–IrishmanSpeaks, is an Irishman, happily exiled in Naperville IL where he says the Guinness is good, the natives are friendly and he has been force-fed more corned beef and green beer than he ever had in Ireland.

He is an internationally recognized keynote speaker, raconteur and Master of Ceremonies whose Brand Promise to clients is **E4**: **E**nergize, **E**ducate, Entertain and **E**asy to work with.

This Irishman has been married to his long suffering wife, Pat, for more years than she cares to remember, and he is proud dad to John and Amy.

Other books by Conor Cunneen:
Why Ireland Never Invaded America
SHEIFGAB! Staying Sane, Motivated and Productive in Job Search
For the Love of Being Irish – An A-Z of Irish History

Keynotes and Presentations include:
The Gift of GAB (Goals, Attitude, Behavior)
Adden Humur two you're Presentashun! (The program is much better than the spelling. Honust!)
Leadership Lessons from Starbucks & Ford Turnarounds
Pillars of Marketing Wisdom
What Mark Twain Learned Me 'bout Public Speakin'
SHEIFGAB! 8 Building Blocks to Improved Productivity, Teamwork and Motivation

You can email Conor at cc@IrishmanSpeaks.com
Twitter: @IrishmanSpeaks www.IrishmanSpeaks.com

"Conor, In almost thirty years of association work, I have never seen a speaker as well received as you."
Incentive Marketing Association

About Mark Twain

The "Dean of American Literature" was born Samuel Langhorne Clemens in Florida, MO in 1835. He left this world a much better place seventy-five years later.

"I came in with Halley's Comet... and I expect to go out with it (in 1910). It will be the greatest disappointment of my life if I don't go out with Halley's Comet. The Almighty has said, "Now here are these two unaccountable freaks; they came in together, they must go out together."

In a life full of much joy, adventure, travel and terrible heartbreak, he was at various times a printer's apprentice, a printer, sometime editor, riverboat pilot (the "only unfettered and entirely independent human being that lived in the earth"), an irregular in the Confederate Army for two weeks and a miner before the first article from Mark Twain appeared in the Nevada *Territorial Enterprise* in 1863.

A level of fame came following the publication of his humorous story *The Celebrated Jumping Frog of Calaveras County* and subsequently some travel reports from the Sandwich Islands (Hawaii.)

A San Francisco lecture in 1866 on his Sandwich Island experiences was the launchpad for an astonishingly successful speaking career. The success of his books *Roughing It, The Adventures of Tom Sawyer, Adventures of Huckleberry Finn* and others allowed him to "retire" from a speaking circuit he had grown tired of.

Unfortunately, his generally atrocious business sense led to bankruptcy and forced the then sixty-year old author into a world speaking tour in 1895 to honor debts even when most creditors were prepared to write them off.

In the last fifteen years of his life, Twain lost his beloved wife and two daughters. Despite the bereavement, he managed to hide his understandable despondent and morose feelings from a public that loved him.

His impact is immeasurable, best summed up by Ernest Hemingway who famously declared in 1935. "All American writing comes from (Huckleberry Finn.) There was nothing before. There has been nothing as good since."

166

Bibliography and Resources

Writing and Works by Mark Twain
Adventures of Huckleberry Finn
The Adventures of Tom Sawyer
Innocents Abroad
Life on the Mississippi
The Prince and the Pauper
Roughing it
Mark Twain Speeches
Joan of Arc
Autobiography of Mark Twain
Mark Twain Letters
Mark Twain in Eruption
The Gilded Age
Following the Equator
The Tragedy of Pudd'nhead Wilson

Other Sources
Paine, Albert Bigelow: Mark Twain – A Biography
Paine, Albert Bigelow: Harper's Magazine
Henderson, Archibald: Mark Twain
Howells, William Dean: My Mark Twain
Merwin, Henry Childs: The Life of Brett Harte

Newspaper Interviews
The Sunday Oregonian
New York Times
New York World
The Seattle Post Intelligencer

Primary Online Resources
MarkTwainProject.com
TwainQuotes.com
Twain.lib.edu
Gutenberg.org

www.ingramcontent.com/pod-product-compliance
Lightning Source LLC
Chambersburg PA
CBHW051652170526
45167CB00001B/437